WRITE FROM THE ST

The Teodorescu Perceptuo-Motor Programme

Developing the fine motor and perceptual
skills for effective handwriting

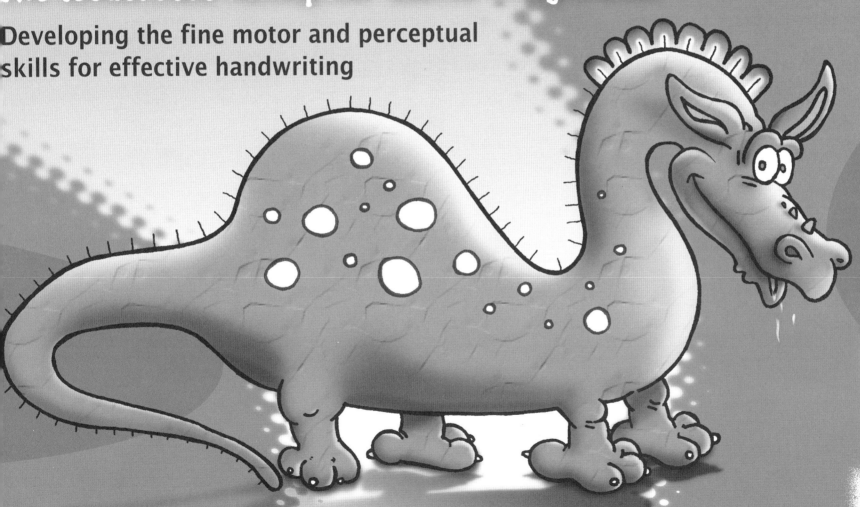

Book 1

Ion Teodorescu
& Lois Addy

Permission to photocopy

This book contains materials which may be reproduced by photocopier or other means for use by the purchaser. The permission is granted on the understanding that these copies will be used within the educational establishment of the purchaser. The book and all its contents remain copyright. Copies may be made without reference to the publisher or the licensing scheme for the making of photocopies operated by the Publishers' Licensing Agency.

The rights of Ion Teodorescu and Lois Addy to be identified as the authors of this work have been asserted by them in accordance with sections 77 and 78 of the Copyright, Designs and Patents Act 1988.

Write from the Start – Book 1
106102
ISBN-13: 978 1 85503 245 3

First published 1996
Reprinted 1997, 1998, 1999, 2000, 2002, 2003, 2004, 2006, 2007, 2009, 2010, 2011, 2012, 2013, 2014, 2015, 2016

Printed in the UK for LDA
Pintail Close, Victoria Business Park,
Nottingham, NG4 2SG UK

Contents

The Authors

Ion Teodorescu was born in Bucharest, Romania in 1953. He was from a small working class family and grew up under the oppressive communist regime which worsened as the megalomania of Ceaucescu's rule became more prominent. Ion Teodorescu was fortunate to attend The University of Bucharest between 1972 and 1976, initially studying Philosophy and Pedagogy. He also studied Romanian culture and was involved in research into human values within education. He has since returned to university to undertake research into childhood literacy.

In 1976 he married and moved to Slobozia in the region of Ialomita, a relatively large town sited between Bucharest and Constanta on the shores of the Black Sea. Here he was allocated to work at a school/orphanage for 250 boys aged between 7 and 17 years. These children were socially and emotionally deprived; many had learning difficulties and some had physical disabilities.

In November 1991 he became director of the school as a result of his commitment and dynamic approach to meet the children's needs.

Write from the Start was developed to assist both the children in his own school and at the local grammar school to develop their handwriting skills. He has also been involved in the introduction and the evaluation of this programme in the UK. His work is only now gaining recognition in his own country.

Lois Addy is a paediatric occupational therapist who has worked within the field of paediatrics for over 20 years. Her particular interest is in the area of visual perception and the associated difficulties experienced by children who have weaknesses in this area.

She has undertaken research into the associated condition of dyspraxia for a number of years while working within a Child Development Centre,

employed by Harrogate Health Care Trust. The evaluation and expansion of the Teodorescu programme has been part of this work. She has also investigated the motivation and learning strategies adopted by children with dyspraxia in comparison with those adopted by non-dyspraxics as well as researching and comparing therapeutic approaches to this condition.

Lois Addy is currently employed as a Senior Lecturer in Professional Health Studies at York St John College, University of Leeds.

She met Professor Teodorescu in 1991 whilst visiting and offering her therapeutic services to the orphanage in which he worked. She retains her link with Romania to date.

Name

The Teodorescu Perceptuo–Motor **Programme**

Ion Teodorescu and Lois M. Addy • A Perceptuo–Motor approach to handwriting

Handwriting booklet 1

Booklet 1

A. Hand–eye co-ordination
Booklet pages 1–3

This is the first stage of the Perceptuo–Motor handwriting programme. It aims to develop the earliest skill in laying foundations for handwriting: hand–eye co-ordination.

Manual control does not simply occur as a result of automatic maturation. Pencil control requires careful practice and experimentation within the various contexts such as colouring, tracking and drawing. Skilled control over movement, as with many other skills requires not only muscle strength, but also an awareness of and sensitivity to various kinds of external feedback, namely proprioception, (awareness of joint position sense) sensory information and the reciprocal balance of muscle tone.

To control a pencil in order to write effectively, a careful balance is needed between muscle tone, co-ordination, proprioception and sensation.

This first exercise serves to develop the control required for exact placement of the pencil on a specified point. It also requires controlled pressure so that the child learns how much to apply in order to make a mark. Alongside this the child learns when to place their hand down onto the page and when to lift it again, thus creating the mark desired.

The natural tendency in this exercise is to join the dots, but this is not the aim; rather it is the precise control of pencil placement.

If a child experiences difficulties in this activity they may prefer to begin this task by using finger paints on the tips of their index fingers, to develop the exact finger-point location. Some children may also find black print on a white background too confusing or distracting and may prefer coloured points on which to focus.

Additional activities have been provided to supplement the exercises.

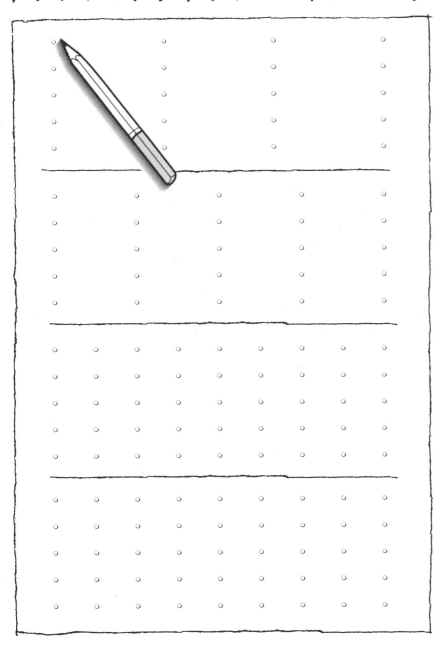

Can you put the freckles on Tom's face?

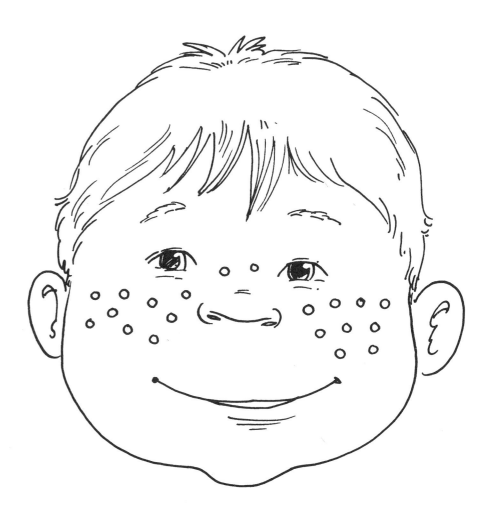

Can you place coloured spots on Dotty's dress?

Can you place coloured spots on Joe's shorts?

Can you place a blue spot on each bubble?

Can you place different coloured spots on the cake?

Booklet 1

B. Form constancy 1
Booklet pages 4–6

These exercises develop an area of perception known as **form constancy**.

Form constancy is the ability to recognise an object despite changes in size, colour, or position. It is because of this area of visual interpretation that we can recognise two and three dimensional forms as being from the same category of shape. For example, a drawing of a square and a cube both belong to the square category of shape.

A person whose perception of form has developed will recognise a cube as a member of the square category even if it is viewed from an oblique angle, as shown here.

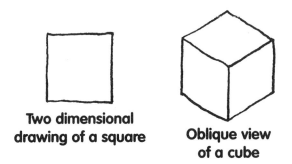

Two dimensional drawing of a square

Oblique view of a cube

A child whose form constancy is dysfunctional may perceive a cube as being a completely different shape to a square. These children will have extreme difficulty matching three dimensional shapes to complete a posting box activity.

Dysfunction in this area will reap serious consequences when learning to write. For example, if a shape of a letter is drawn on the blackboard, the child may perceive this differently when attempting to reproduce the same shape on paper.

The exercises which follow will assist the child to experience the form of a circle, but additional activities involving touch and movement are necessary to establish the understanding of form, for example: feeling the shape of a plate, or the outline of a ball or steering wheel.

These exercises help the child to feel the movement required to produce a circle.

The child is taught to create a circle by repeatedly following an outline. Initially they form what looks like circular scribble, but gradually by the fluent movements required, and using the circular boundary given, the shape is organised to resemble a clear circle.

As the child progresses through the circles they should begin to see that the beginning of the circle should join with the end, ultimately without being able to see the join.

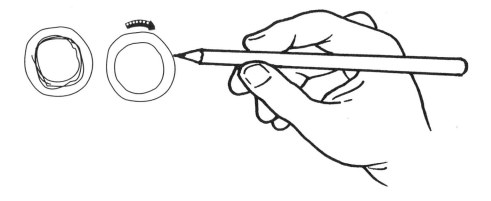

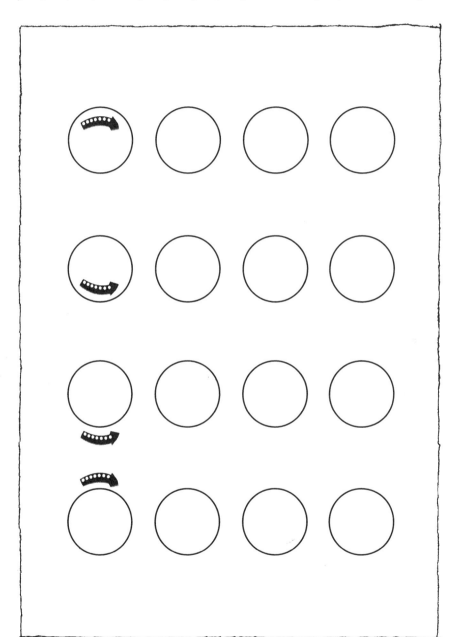

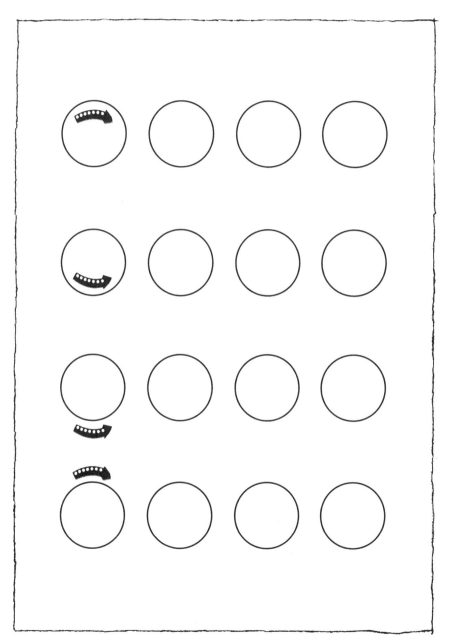

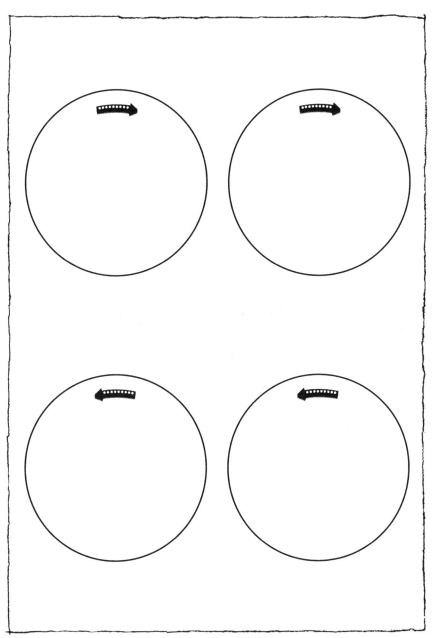

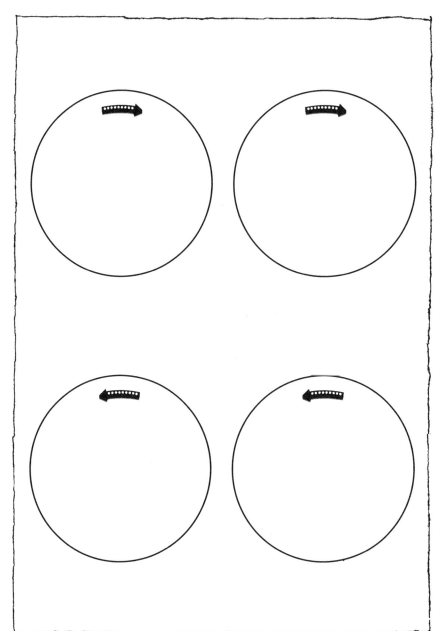

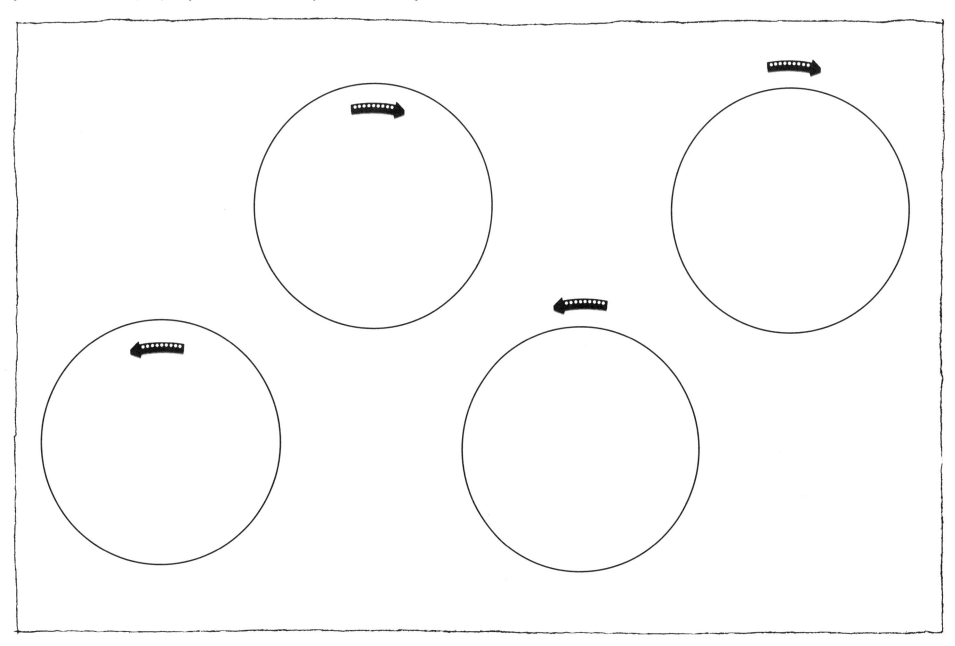

Booklet 1

C. Form constancy 2
Booklet pages 7–9
Additional worksheets 10–13

Progressing from the previous exercise which involved the creation of circles using bold guidelines, the next series of tasks involves the creation of circular movements when given punctuated lines to guide the pencil. Once this has been mastered in both clockwise and anticlockwise directions, the size of the circle is decreased.

The aim of this task is to further the child's understanding of form. It also promotes experimentation with orientation.

Further forms are then introduced to develop an awareness of other shapes such as triangles and squares. These are produced both inside and outside the stencil of the shape provided, as shown here.

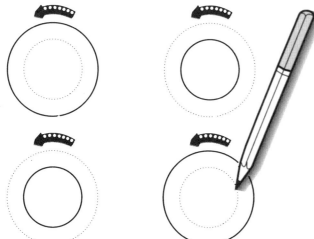

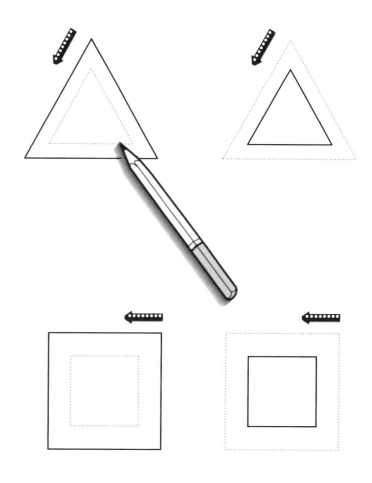

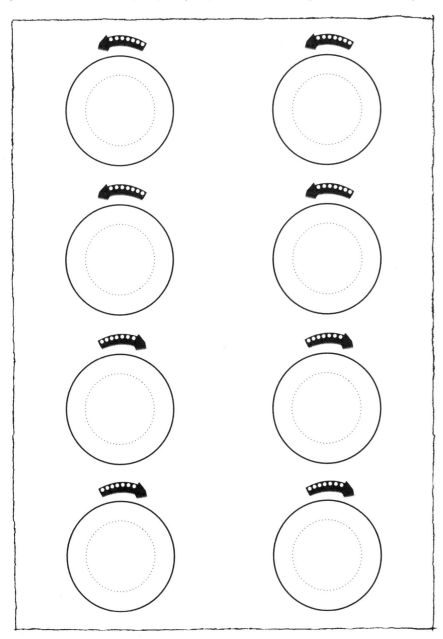

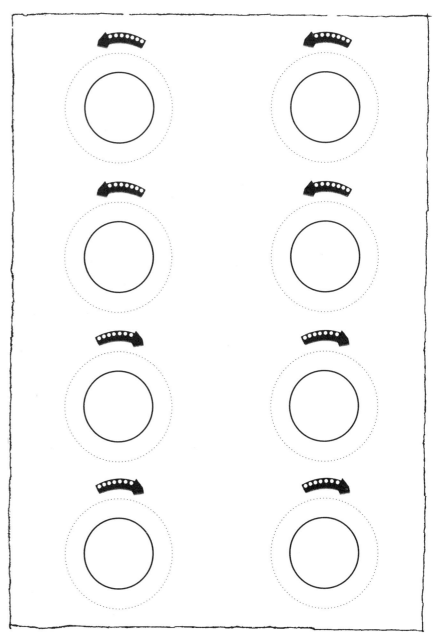

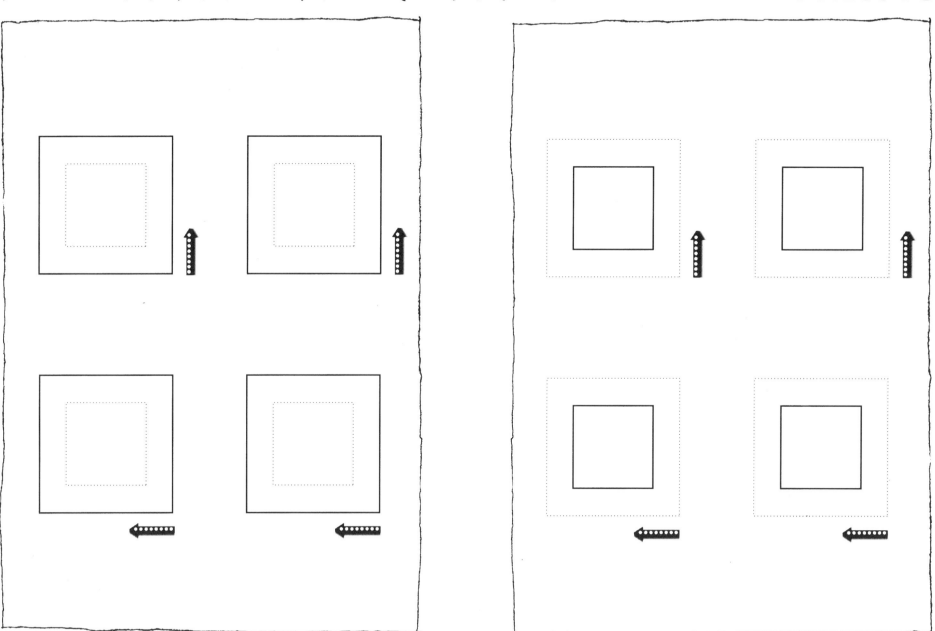

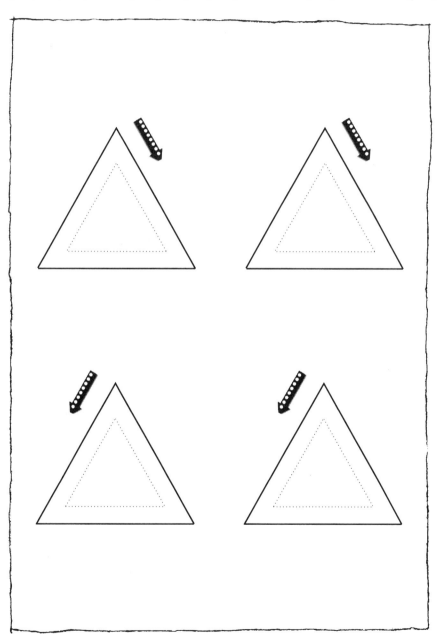

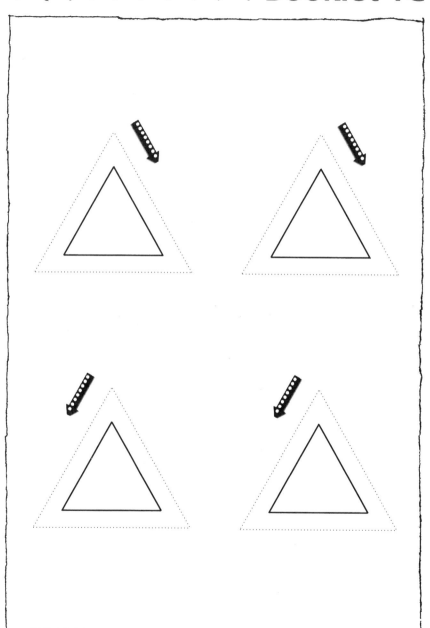

Can you draw around the bubbles?

Can you draw around the baby's building blocks?

Can you draw around the triangles in this picture?

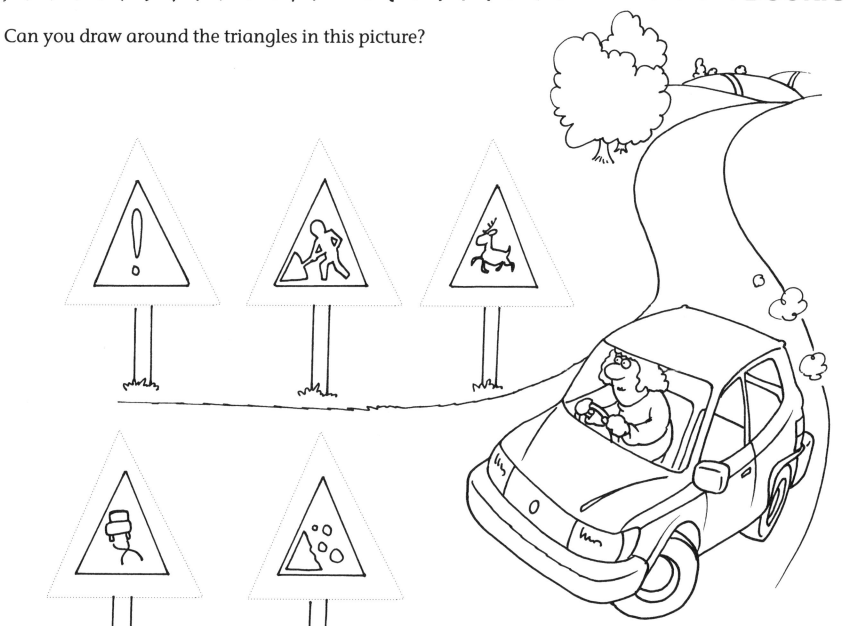

Can you draw around the circles,
squares and triangles in this picture?

Can you draw yourself watching the circus?

Name

The Teodorescu Perceptuo–Motor **Programme**

Ion Teodorescu and Lois M. Addy • A Perceptuo–Motor approach to handwriting

Handwriting booklet 2

Booklet 2

A. Form recognition and motor control
Booklet pages 1–5

Now that the child has experienced the shape and formation of circles, triangles and squares, this section serves to take the discovery of form perception one step further. It introduces **figure–ground discrimination**.

The child is asked to place a circle inside, then outside squares and triangles. The natural tendency is for the child to produce a square shape within the square, and a triangular shape within the triangle, as shown here.

The child must learn to differentiate between the various shapes and understand the variations in the form.

The shapes given are deliberately small at first, focusing the child's vision on a very narrow area. This visual field is then expanded through the introduction of larger shapes. The intrinsic muscles of the hand are also developed: a necessary requisite for accurate letter formation.

Ensure that the child always follows the direction of the arrows so that ability to vary direction is developed. Observation will reveal the child's understanding of orientation and also whether perception in this area is impaired or delayed.

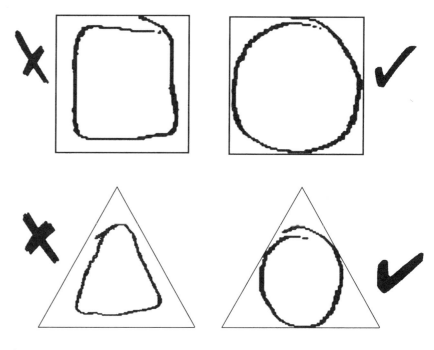

Circles inside and outside squares and triangles

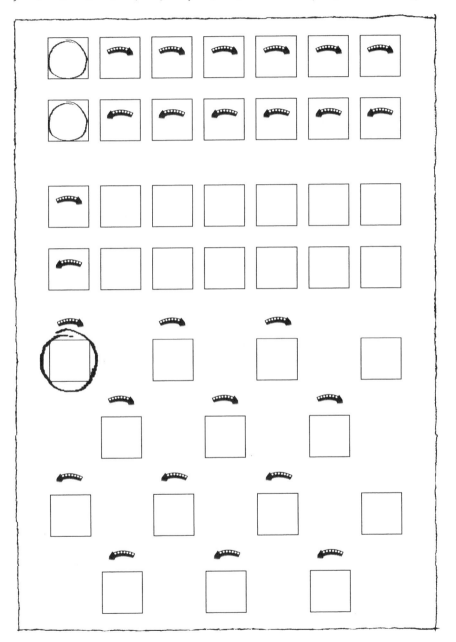

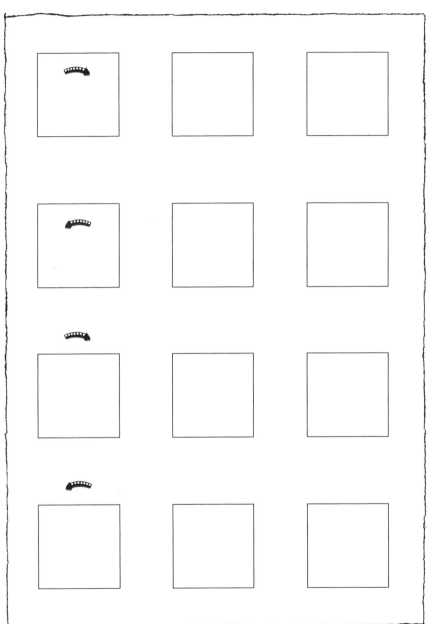

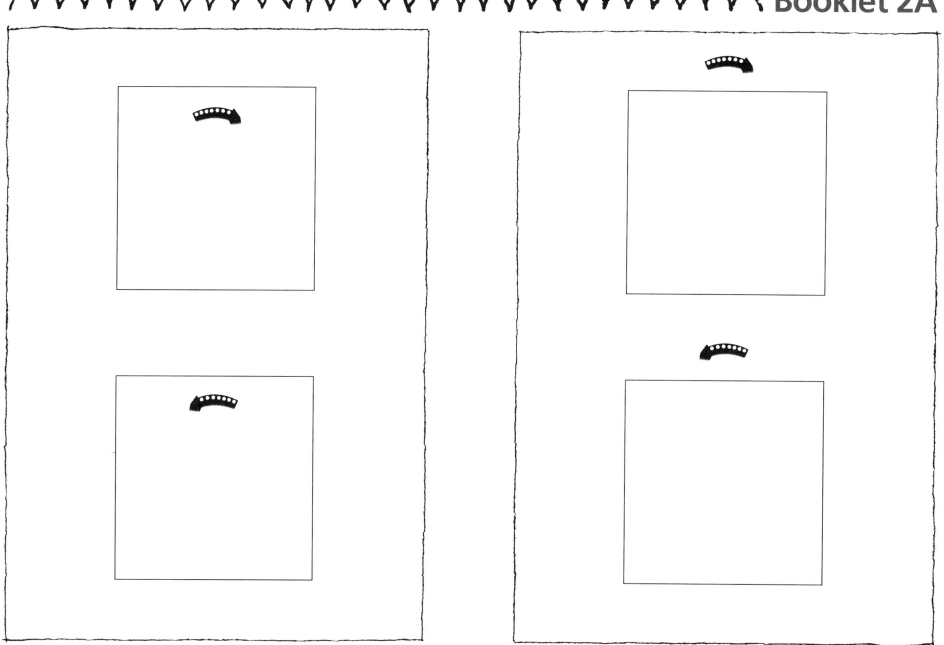

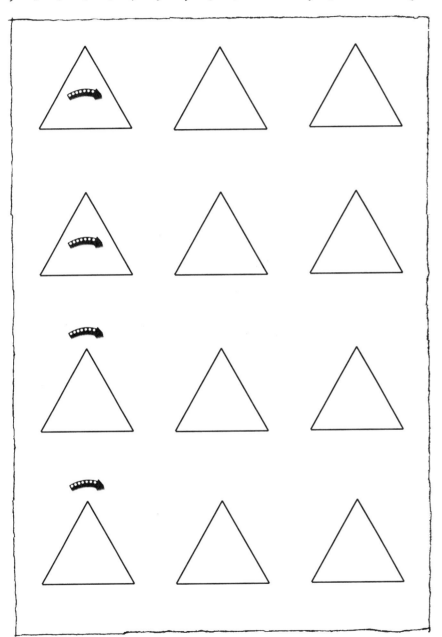

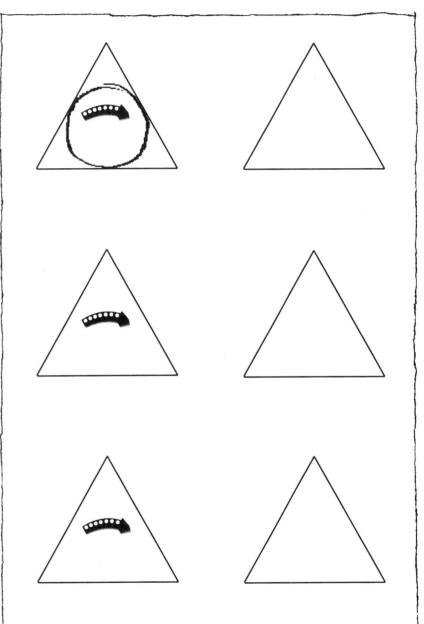

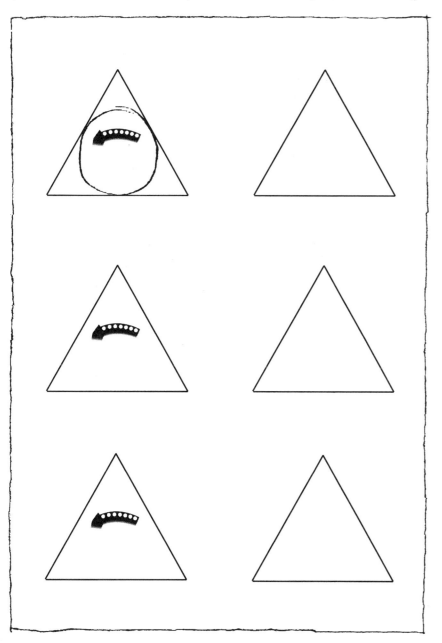
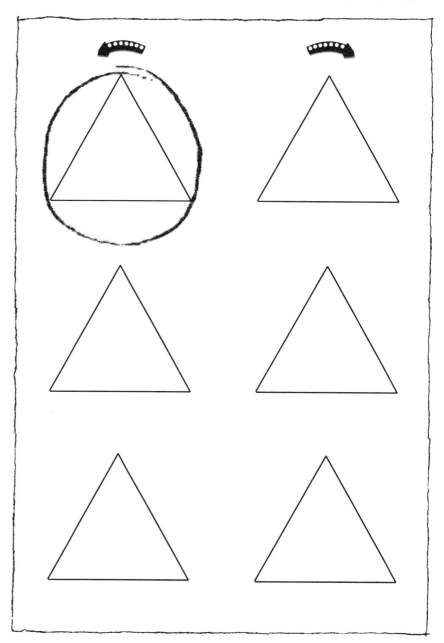

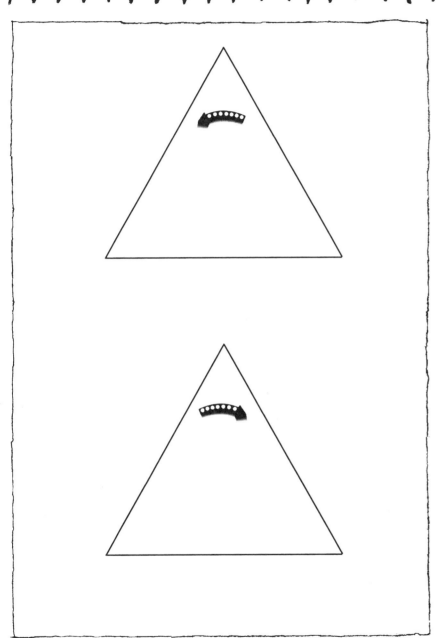

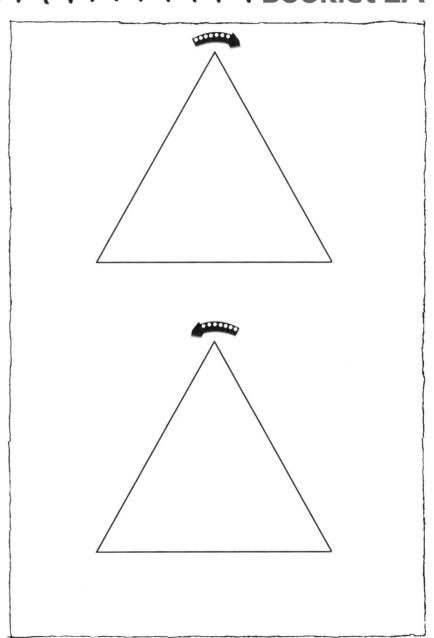

Booklet 2

B. Spatial judgement
Booklet pages 6–10
Additional worksheets 11–13

The following exercises are known in Romania as 'the tail of the dragon', the patterns symbolising the spines on a dragon's back.

These exercises aim to develop the child's awareness of space. This is fundamental when learning that words are made up of individual letters which, when grouped together, form meaningful words. This understanding is an essential component in the development of a child's handwriting.

The child is encouraged to 'jump' over each spine with their pencil without stopping. They will probably struggle with the dilemma of how to continue the pattern when confronted by an angle or turn. For this, they will need to learn how to adjust their position, grasp and pencil tension to accommodate the change in direction.

The child's spatial organisation is promoted by the need to make a mental judgement of the distances to be jumped and then accommodating these distances by means of pencil control. The spaces between the spines are graduated as the exercises become more complex. Where the spines are placed on both aspects of the central line the child must jump across the spines from left to right and then continue around the corner to return to the left as shown here.

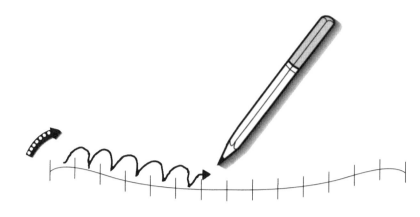

Jumping over the spines

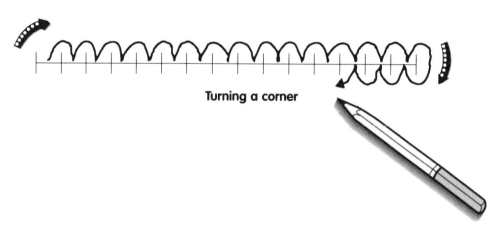

Turning a corner

If a child finds real difficulty with these exercises they may be helped by additional activities such as suggested in the supplementary activities section.

If a child has specific difficulties in viewing black on white, the base line can be overlined using a coloured pen to clarify direction and base.

Supplementary activities

Fill a tray with fine sand and place small blocks in a row in the tray. Guide the child's index finger through the sand or foam, jumping over the blocks. Remove the blocks to reveal the resultant pattern.

1 The child can then practise this independently in the sand, encouraging the fluency required to undertake the exercises within the programme. You could also try this activity with hypoallergenic shaving foam.
2 Shade a blackboard with chalk, placing coloured crosses equally spaced in a row across the board. The child can then track across the board, jumping over each cross using a wetted index finger.
3 Use the additional worksheets to develop control prior to tackling the exercises in this section.

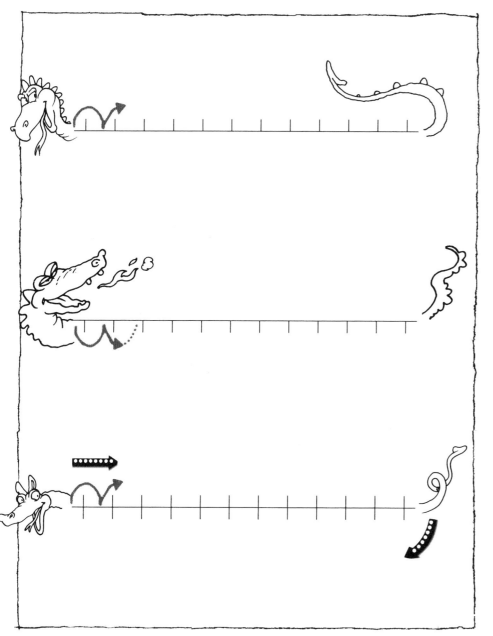

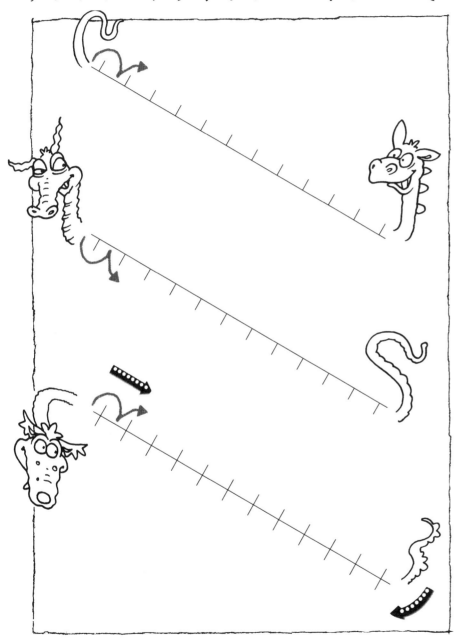

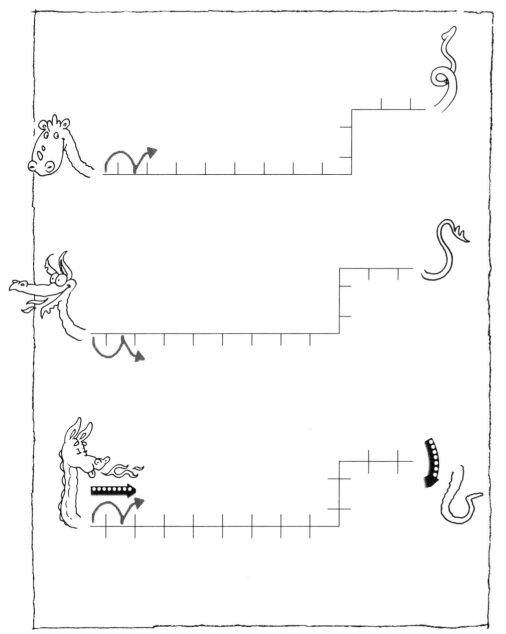

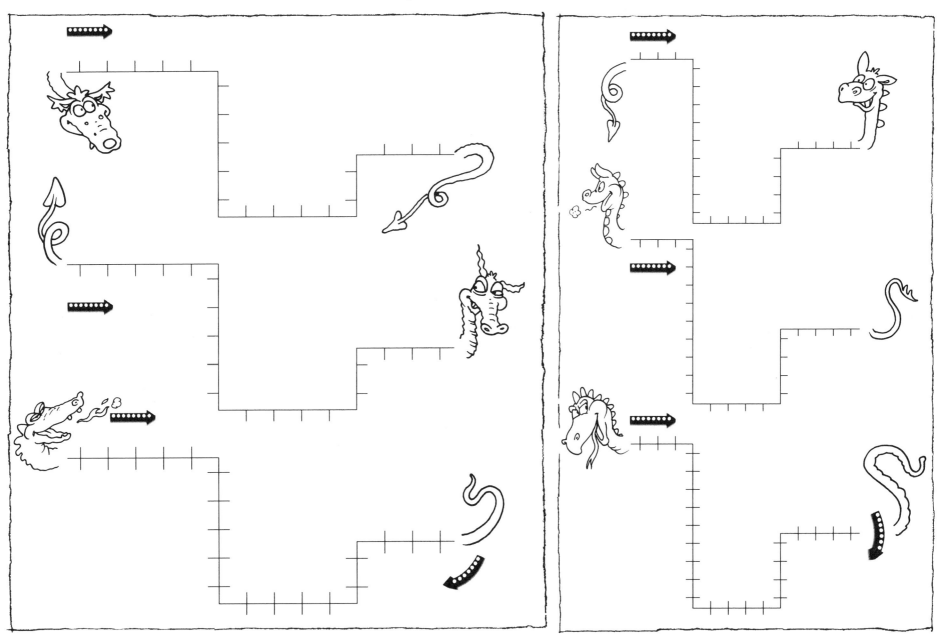

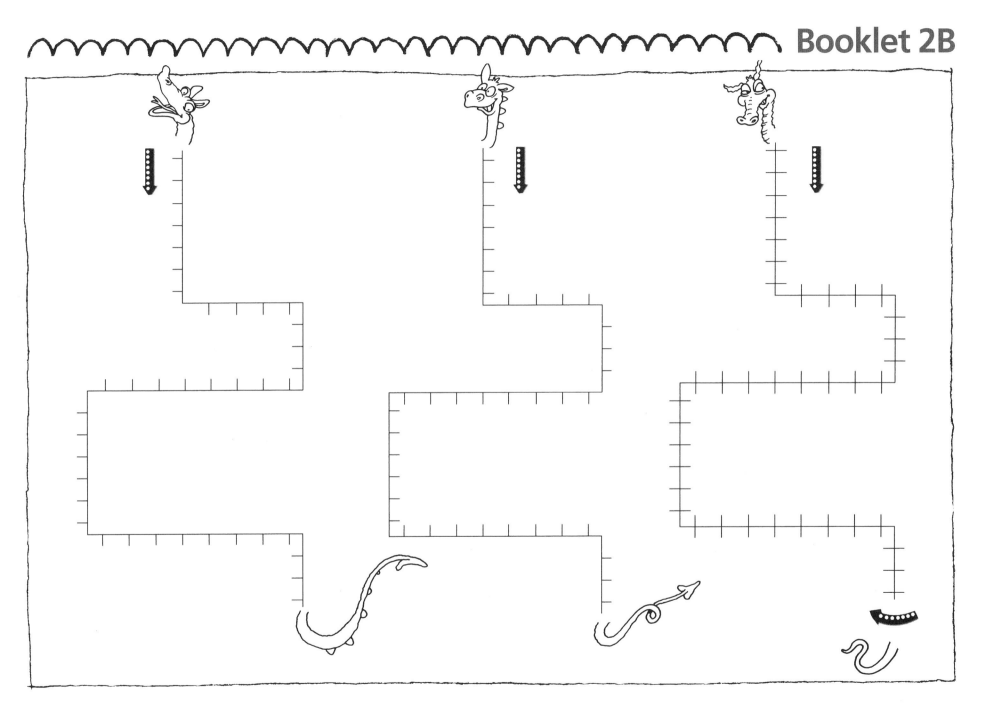

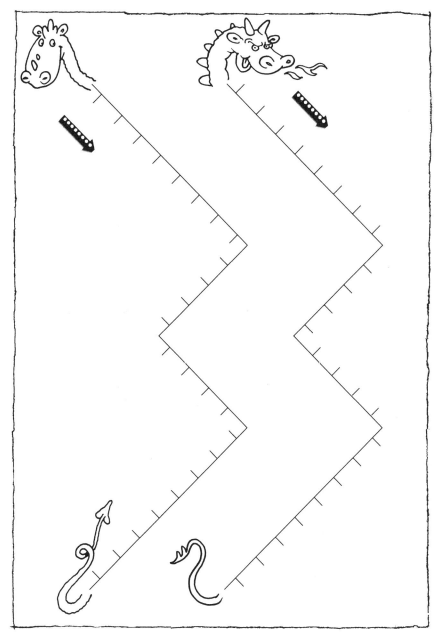

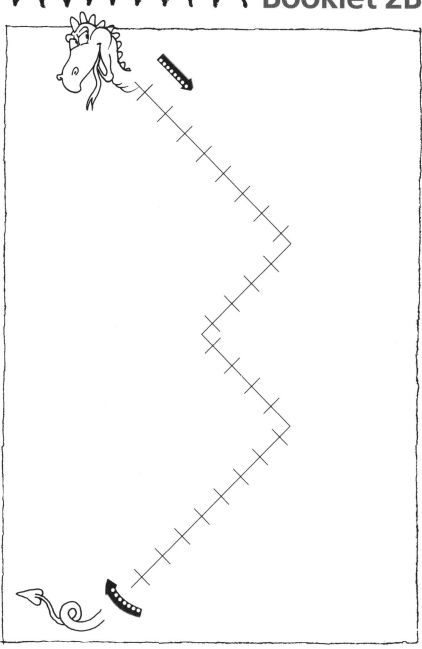

Can you draw the spines on the dragon's back?

Now can you colour in the dragon?

Can you make the frog jump across the lily pads?

Can you give the snake a pattern?

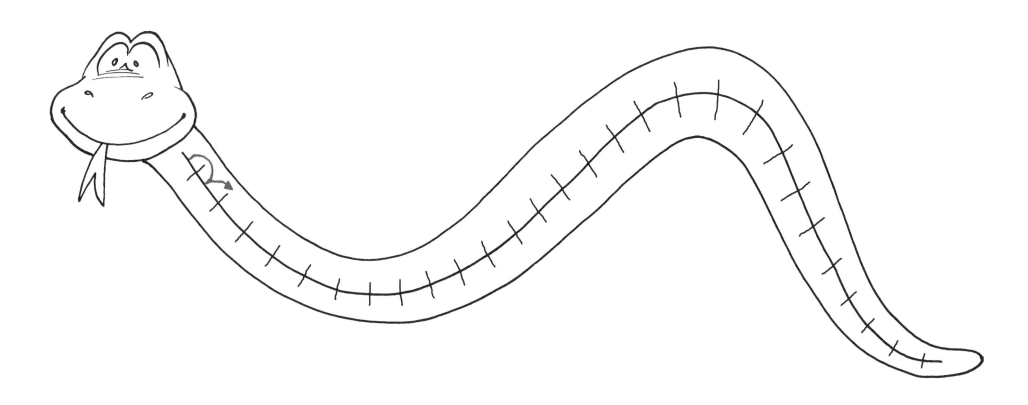

Now colour in the pattern.

Name

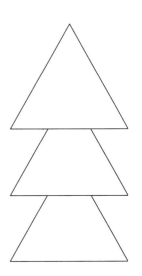

The Teodorescu Perceptuo-Motor **Programme**

Ion Teodorescu and Lois M. Addy • A Perceptuo–Motor approach to handwriting

Start

→

End

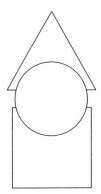

Handwriting booklet 3

Booklet 3

A. Linear control

These exercises encourage the child to control the pencil along the horizontal and vertical plane. It teaches the child that every line or pencil mark has a beginning and an end, reinforcing the need to control the production of letter forms, and seeing the commencement and conclusion of each letter, or word.

These exercises introduce the left to right orientation necessary in British literacy, and this is highlighted by the arrows provided at the start of each task.

The child must place their pencil on the starting point and then follow the given reference points to the end. The important aspect of this is the ability to scan carefully from the starting point to the final position, without overshooting to the edge of the page. As the exercises progress, fewer guidance points are given until ultimately the child can draw a line from the left side of the page to the right without the need for intermediate referencing, as shown by the examples here.

Page 7 has a similar focus but the line is controlled in a vertical direction either from the top downwards or bottom upwards. The control of curves, practised in Booklets 1 & 2, and straight lines as in this Booklet, provide the fundamental movements required to produce effective letter formation.

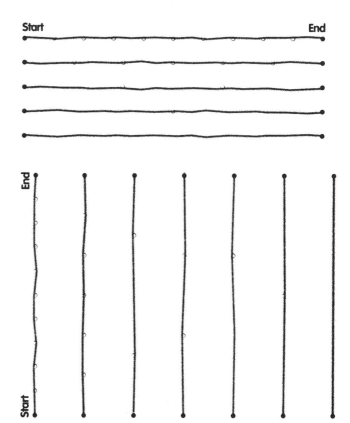

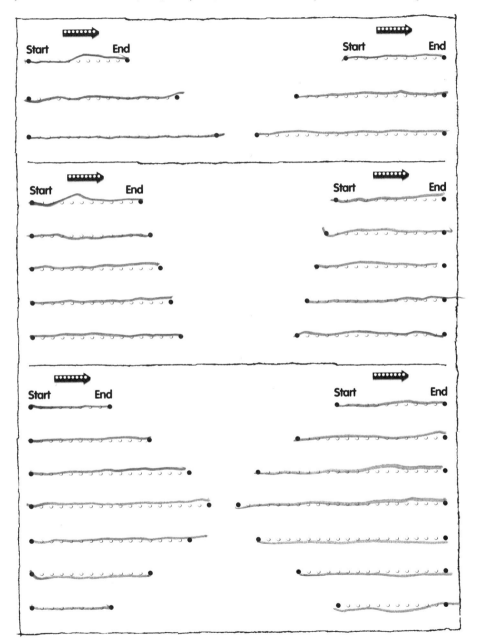

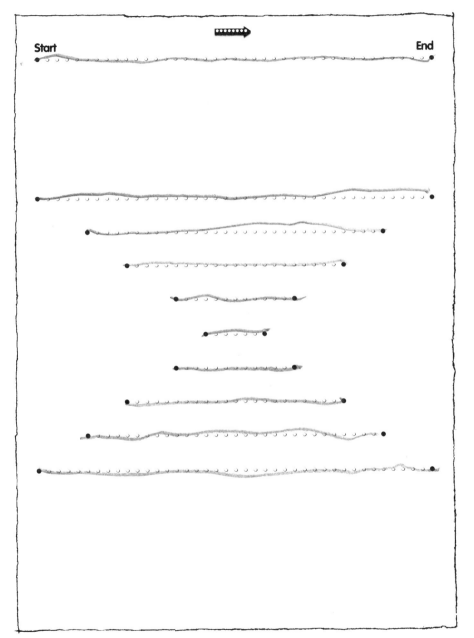

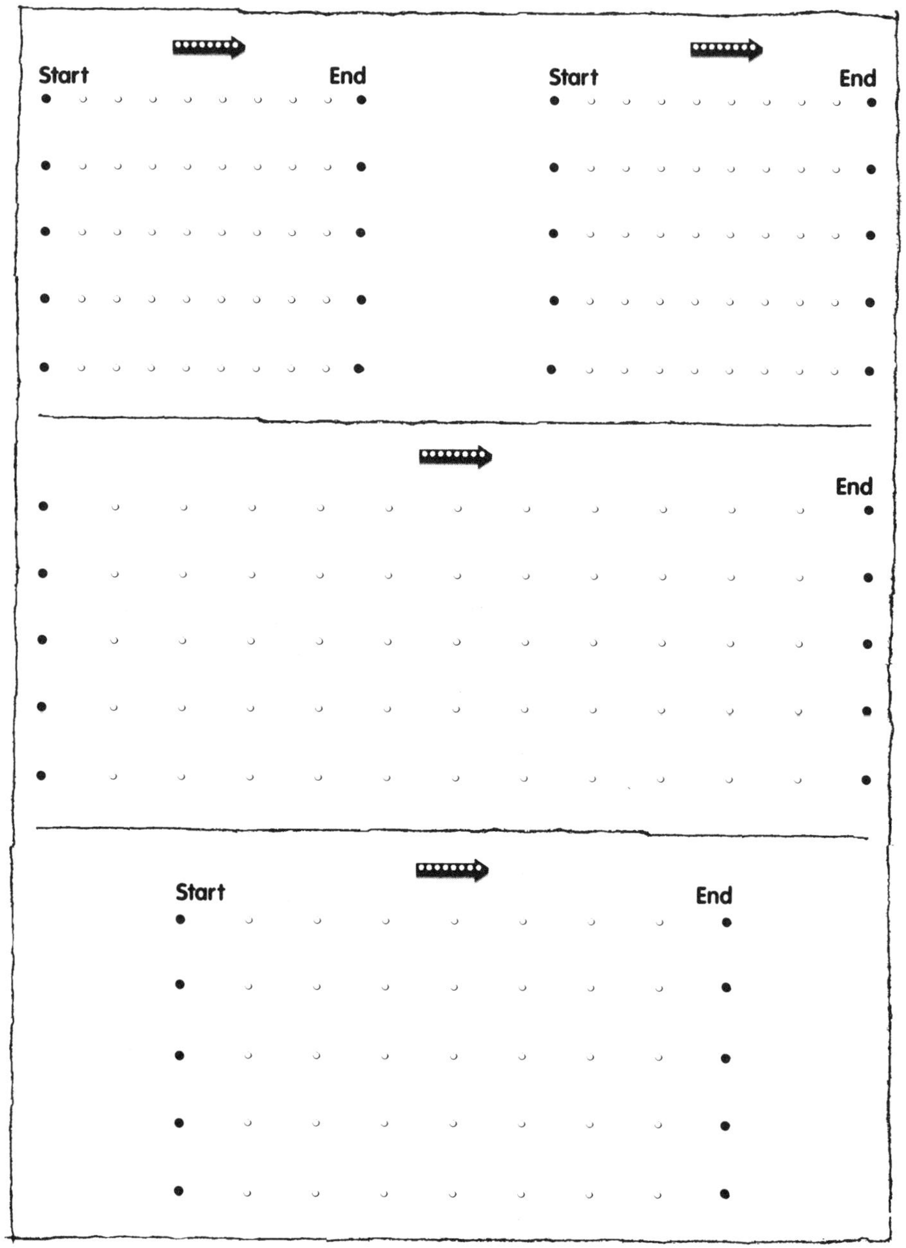

Start   End   Start   End

Start   End   Start   End

End

Start   End

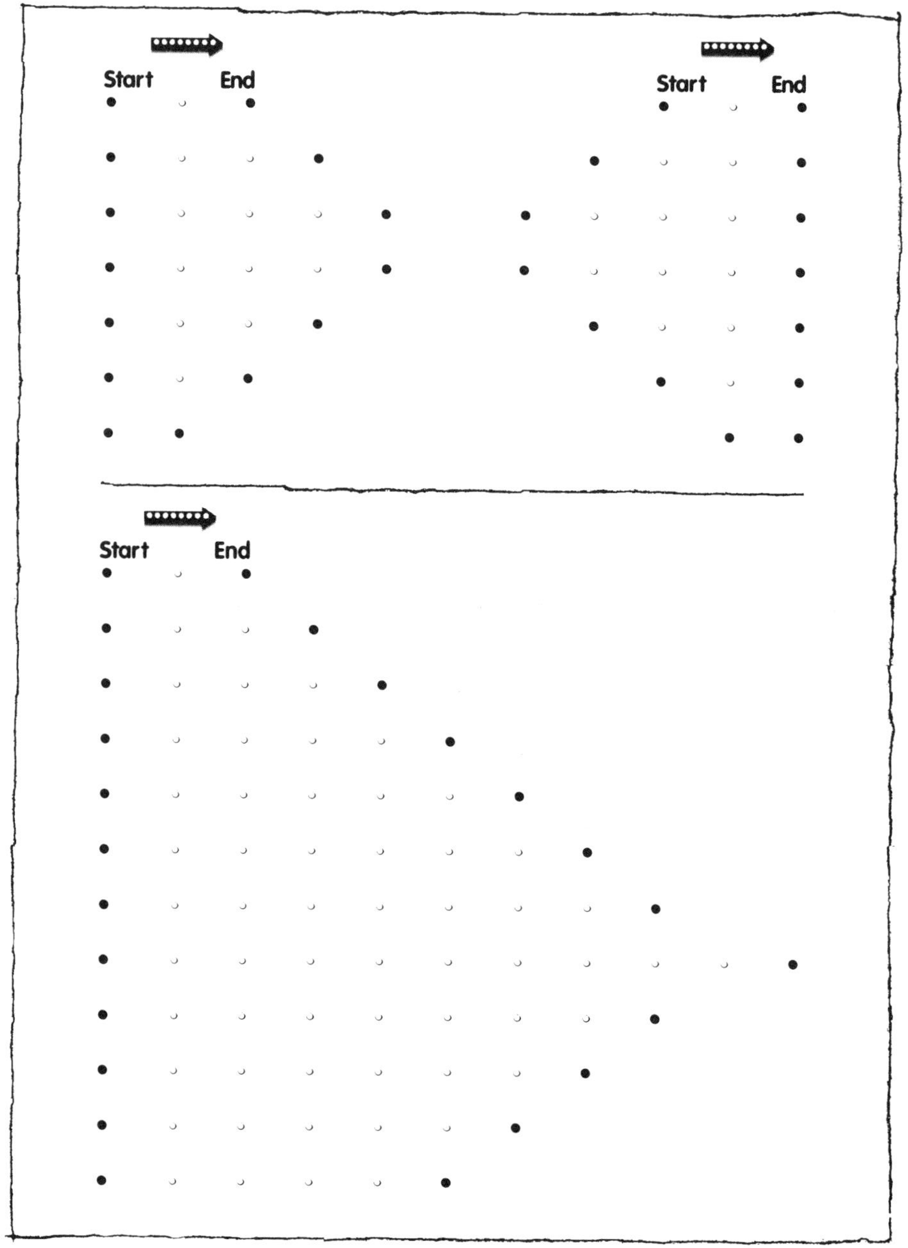

Start   End

Start   End

Start   End

Start   End

Start   End

Start   End

Start   End

Start   End

Start   End

Start   End

Start   End

Start   End

Start   End

Start   End   Start   End

Start   End

Start   End

Start   End

Start   End

Start   End

Start   End

Start   End

Start

End

Start

End

End

Start

End

Start

Booklet 3

B. Figure–ground discrimination
Booklet pages 8–12
Additional worksheets 13–20

This is an extremely interesting series of exercises which tests and develops the child's understanding of **figure–ground discrimination**.

Figure–ground discrimination is the ability to differentiate visually between an object or item which we perceive to be in the foreground and that which is in the background. We focus on that which is important without being distracted by the environment. The human brain is amazing in its ability to select specific information from the mass of incoming stimuli in the form of colour, light, form and noise. For example, a child is able to focus on the blackboard despite the distracting stimuli of wall montages, mobiles, displays, other classmates, noise and smells, in a busy classroom because of their astute figure–ground discrimination.

The figure or object is at that time, the centre of the observer's attention. When the observer shifts his attention to something else, a new focus evolves, the previous focus fading into the background.

A child with distorted figure–ground discrimination will present as being disorganised, 'in a perpetual muddle,' easily distracted and inattentive. This is due to their inability to focus on the essential figure, and consequent distraction by the mass of stimuli around them.

For this reason, the following exercises are both experimental and experiential for the child, and diagnostic to the teacher or therapist.

The child should be given five or six coloured pencils and asked to colour first the shape at the 'front' of the picture. The exercises with the circles demonstrate the variety of ways the shapes can be stacked. The child colours the remainder of the pictures, deciding for themself how the shapes should be treated.

By observing how each child tackles the exercises will give some indication as to how that child is distinguishing the 'figure' from its 'background'. Further exercises are provided to assist and reinforce this area of perception.

Figure–ground discrimination is of specific importance to handwriting in enabling children to recognise letter forms within words. Without it, children find it difficult to focus on producing an individual letter form, being visually distracted by the shapes of other letter forms as they do so.

Supplementary activities

Object discrimination
This game can be played with the whole class, a small group, or individual children. Say to the child, 'Bring me an object in the room which is round.'

Further items can be requested relating to:

Colour: 'Bring me something in the room which is blue.'

Shape: 'Bring me something in the room which is square.'

Texture: 'Bring me something in the room which is smooth.'

Weight: 'Bring me something in the room which is heavy.'

Sorting activities
Find a square button hidden amongst a box of round buttons.
Find a small block hidden in a box full of large blocks.
Find a green marble hidden in a box full of blue marbles.

Find all the pigs in a tray full of farmyard animals.

Find all the blue cars in a box full of mixed objects.

Have objects of two or more types together and ask the children to sort them in terms of:
- size
- colour
- shape
- texture.

Looking activity books
Use activity books that require the child to find certain items hiding within the pages. For example:

Puzzle Town, Puzzle Farm, Puzzle Island. Usborne

Where's Wally? and *Where's Wilma?* Walker Books

Word searches and object grids
Grids which incorporate words or objects hidden in various directions – horizontal, vertical, reversed, or diagonally placed. Some examples are provided in the additional work sheets.

Overlapping objects
Given pictures of interlocking shapes and objects, the child must identify each shape by outlining or marking the object. Several examples are provided in the additional worksheets.

Let's Look, LDA, provides a photocopiable resource of visual discrimination activity sheets.

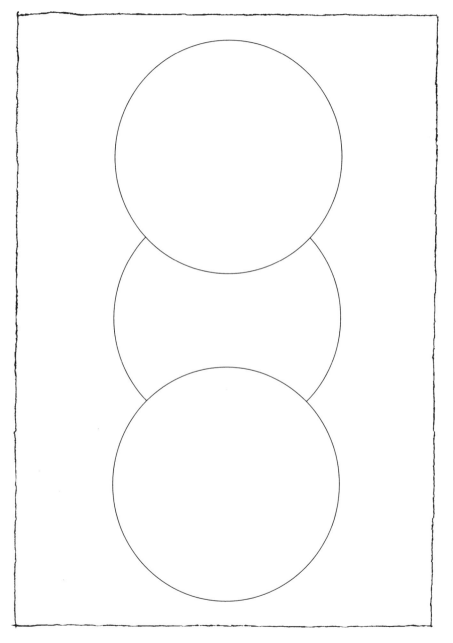

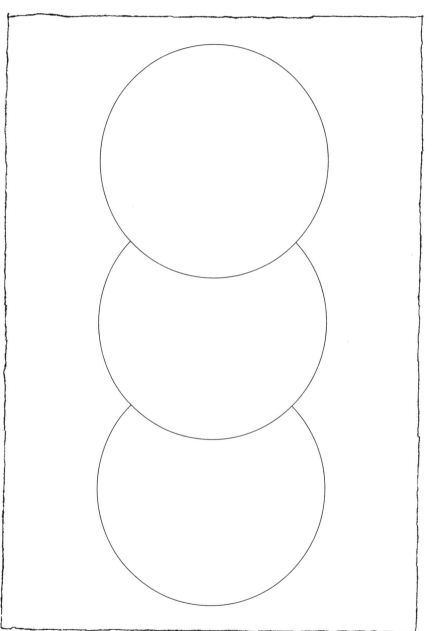

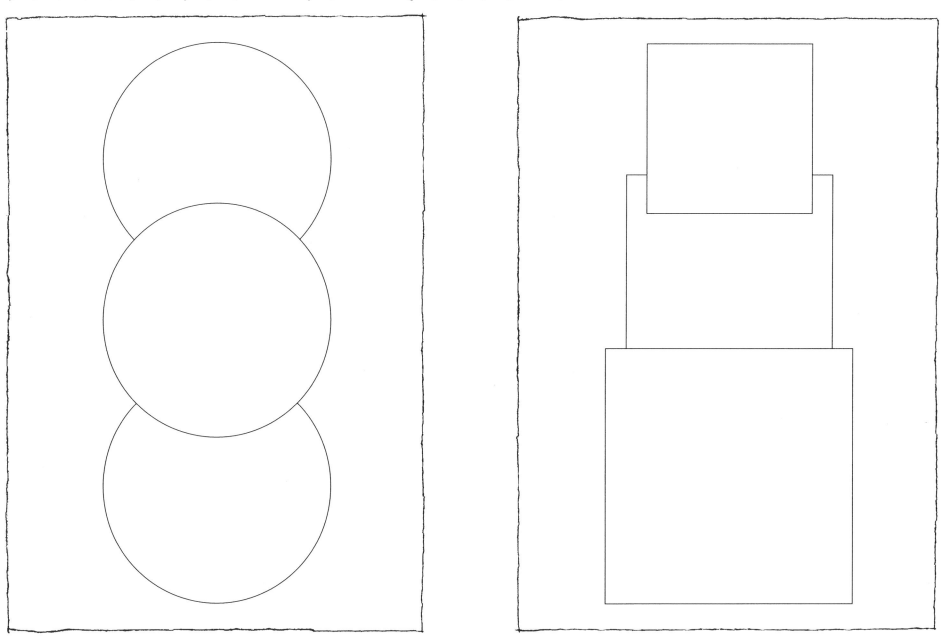

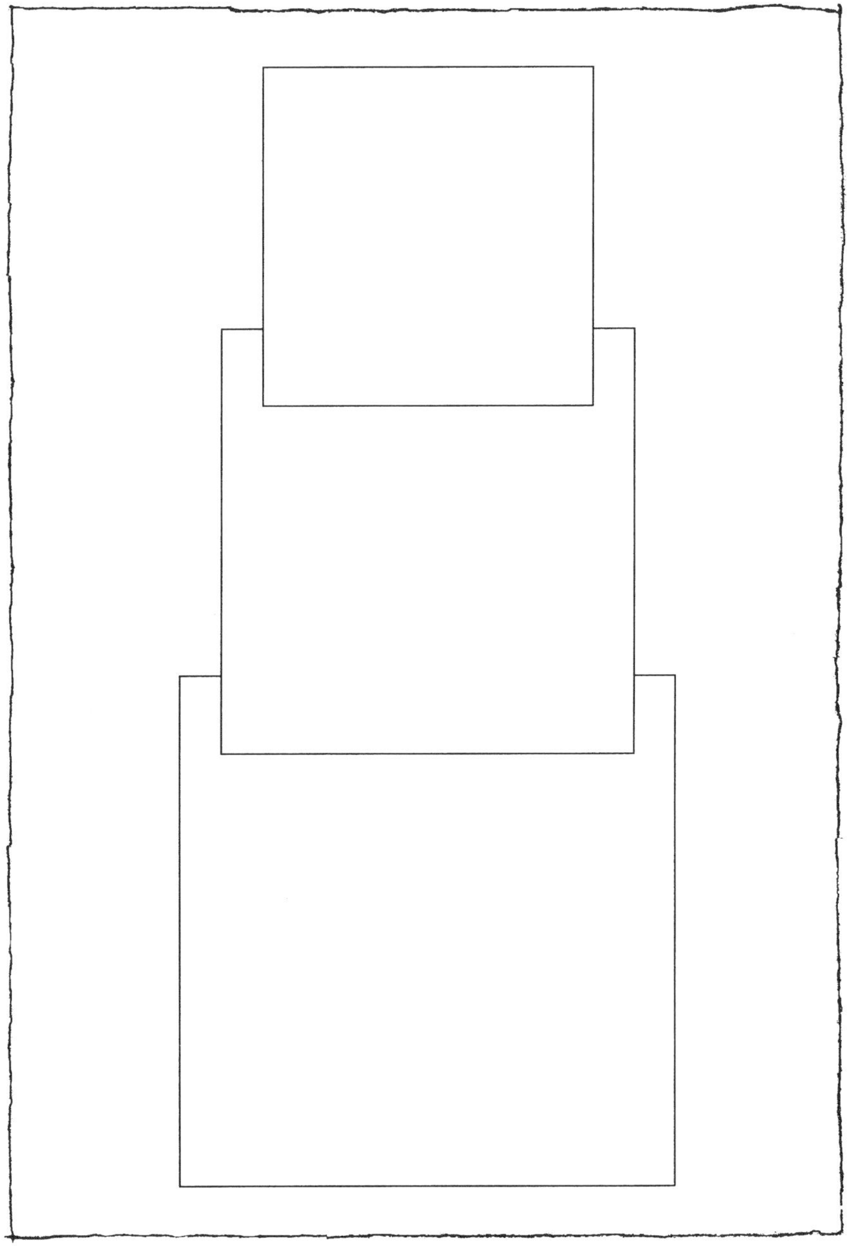

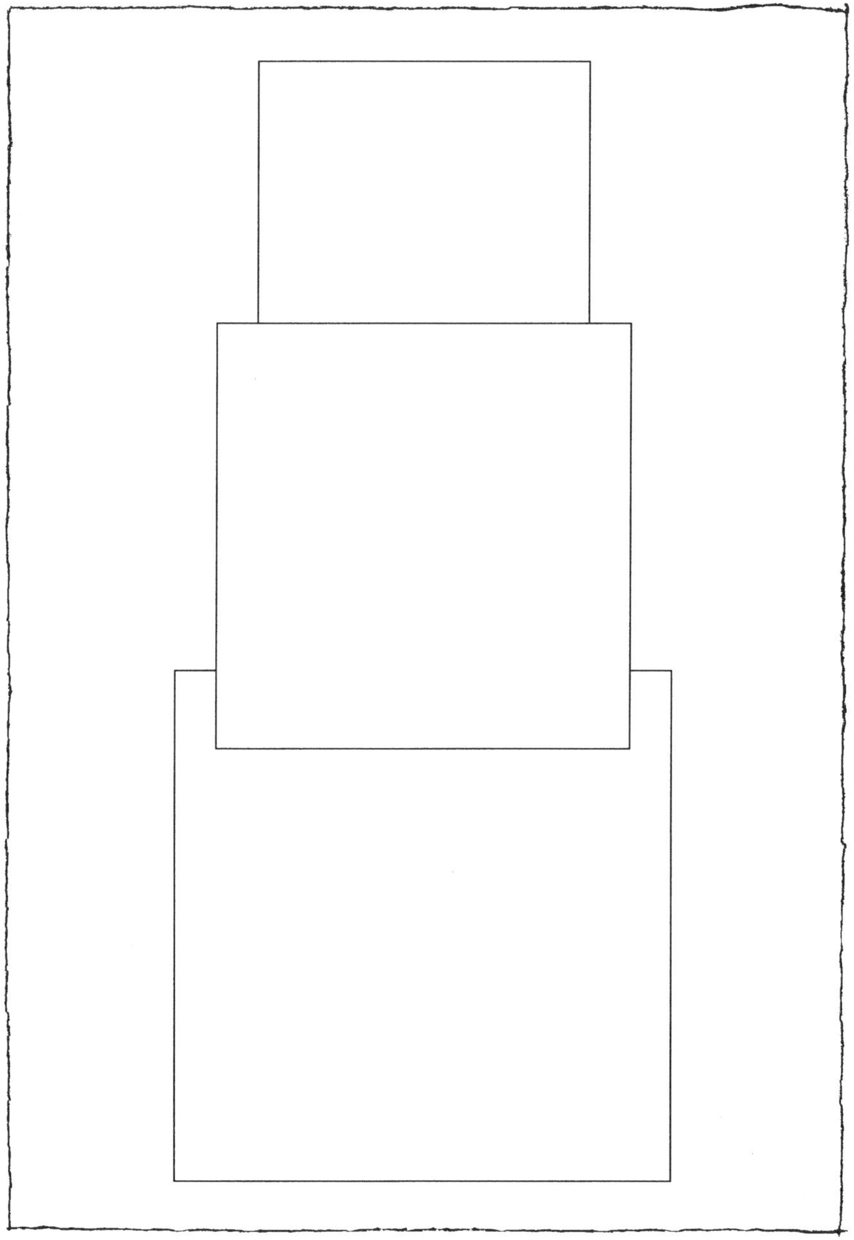

Find the fruit

 colour green

 colour orange

 colour red

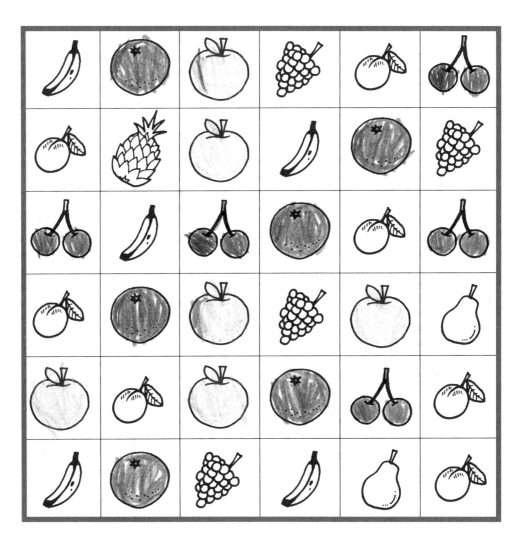

Mark all the

 in blue

 in red

 in green

 in yellow

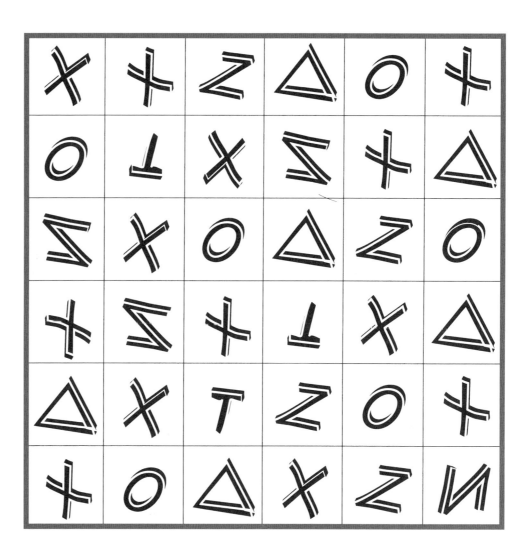

Can you find these words hidden in the grid?

boy
dog
see
log
toy
bus
book
bee
hut

b	o	y	g	o	b
l	d	s	e	e	d
t	o	g	l	o	g
o	g	t	b	u	s
b	o	o	k	h	y
y	t	y	t	u	h
h	b	e	e	t	t
s	e	o	g	e	n

Can you find these colours hidden in the grid?

red
blue
green
orange
black
yellow
brown
purple
pink
white

k	n	i	p	a	o	r	n	e	g
b	l	e	w	o	w	b	e	d	r
e	n	p	u	r	p	l	e	y	e
y	w	l	l	e	o	u	l	g	l
p	o	r	e	d	r	e	p	r	l
e	r	u	o	r	a	n	g	e	e
t	b	r	g	w	o	l	l	e	y
i	r	b	l	a	c	k	b	n	l
h	a	e	n	l	b	n	w	l	o
w	c	e	k	e	y	r	o	r	w

Can you find these words hidden in the grid?

daddy
car
train
school
lorry
table
sister
flag
kitten
house

Can you colour each thing from the woods?

Can you colour each thing from the seaside?

Can you colour each thing from the toy shop?

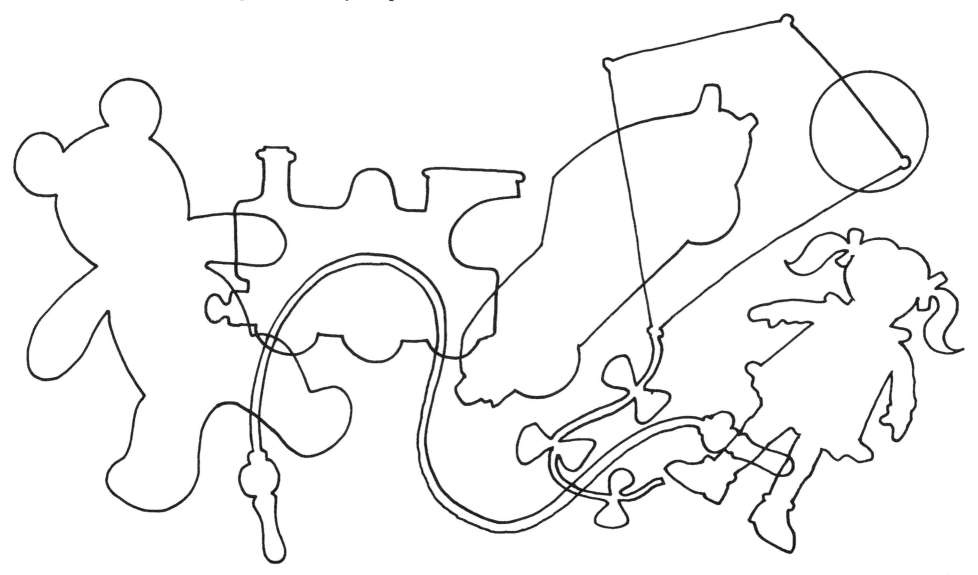

Booklet 3

C. Visual closure
Booklet pages 21–25

This series of exercises summarises the tasks completed so far. It develops hand–eye co-ordination, form constancy and, additionally, an area of perception known as **visual closure**.

Visual closure is the ability to identify an object even though its outline has been fragmented. The parts come together to enable the whole (the gestalt) to be seen

This assists the child in understanding that each letter, although representative on its own, has meaning when placed together with others to form a word. This can be seen in the examples given.

This is the reason why the use of cursive (joined) writing from an early age is important. If the child is shown how a letter form appears in the context of a word, then a connection is made in the perception of a word as a unit and not a series of fragmented drawings. This, along with the development of fluency, direction and orientation enables the child to make a smooth progression from patterning to the fluent patterns needed in writing.

When printing, individual letters are 'drawn'.

m n a e s k t u

w b o l d f

But when the letters are demonstrated individually and then shown within the context of a word, then the gestalt of the word is perceived. This helps the child to understand spaces between words, alignment, and page organisation.

e ee leek see
o oo look too
a car man

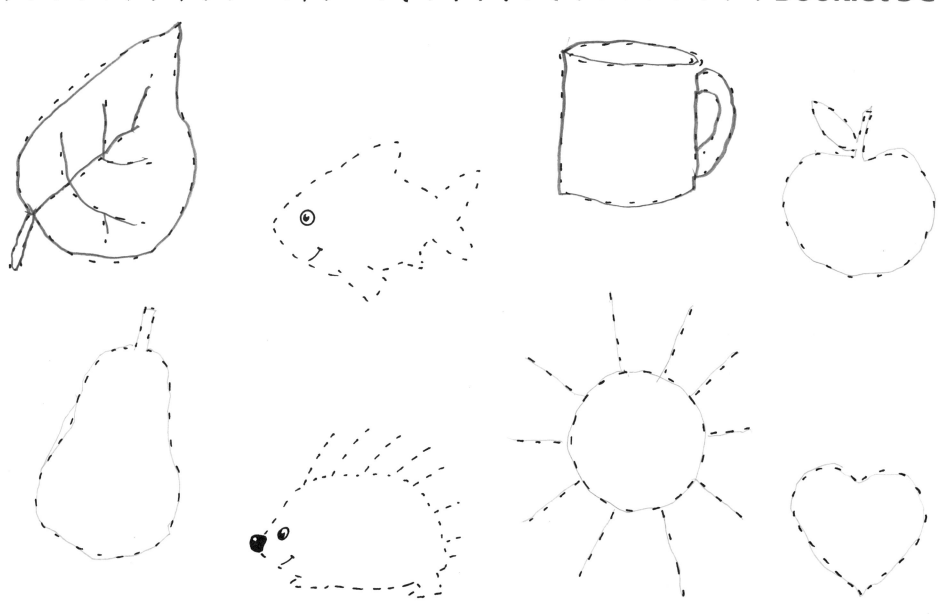

Can you join the lines to see the animal?

Can you join the lines to see a cartoon character?

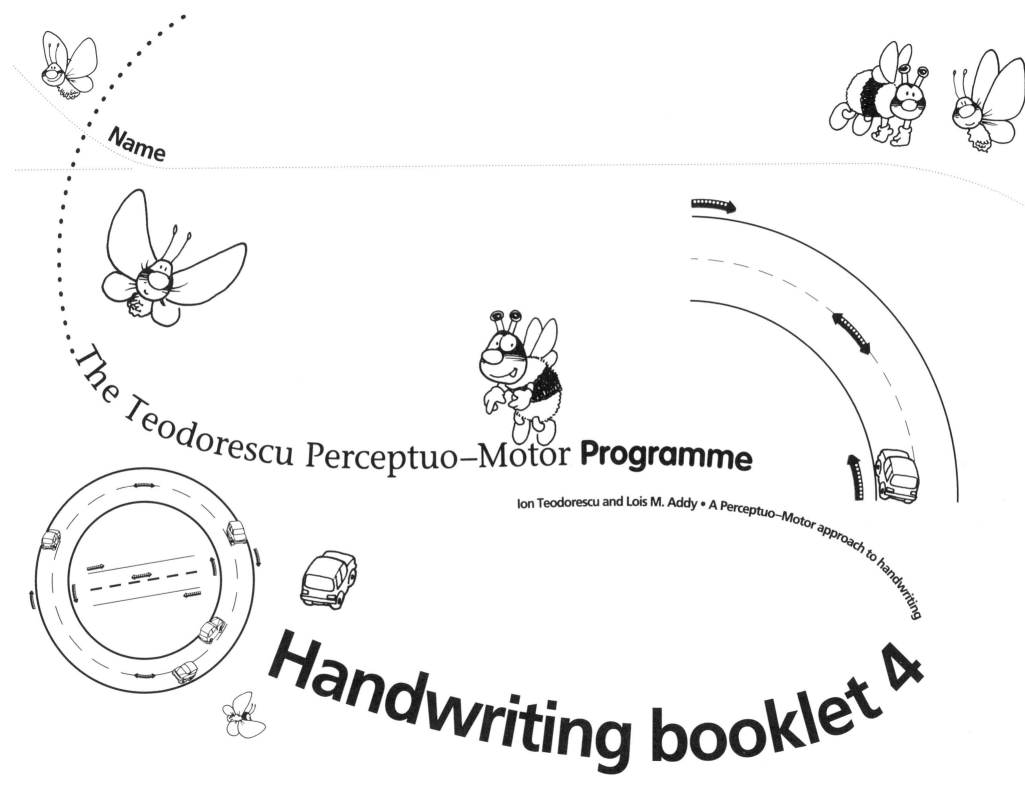

Name

The Teodorescu Perceptuo–Motor **Programme**

Ion Teodorescu and Lois M. Addy • A Perceptuo–Motor approach to handwriting

Handwriting booklet 4

Booklet 4

A. Orientation

This series of exercises serves to develop the perception of directionality. 'Roads' are given to travel along.

The solid lines must be followed in the direction of the arrow. The fragmented line allows the child to choose whichever direction they prefer. In this way the child explores their comfort in orientating from left to right or from right to left.

It is worthwhile observing the direction chosen by the child as this will indicate their maturation. Children who prefer to track from right to left may find a particular difficulty in the orientation of letters, preferring to form them in a clockwise direction rather than anticlockwise. This is especially prevalent in left-handers.

A child with this difficulty may also prefer to commence writing at the right side of a page and may 'mirror write'.

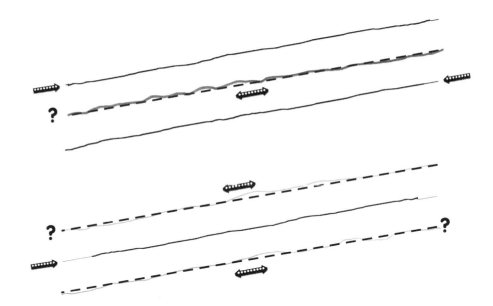

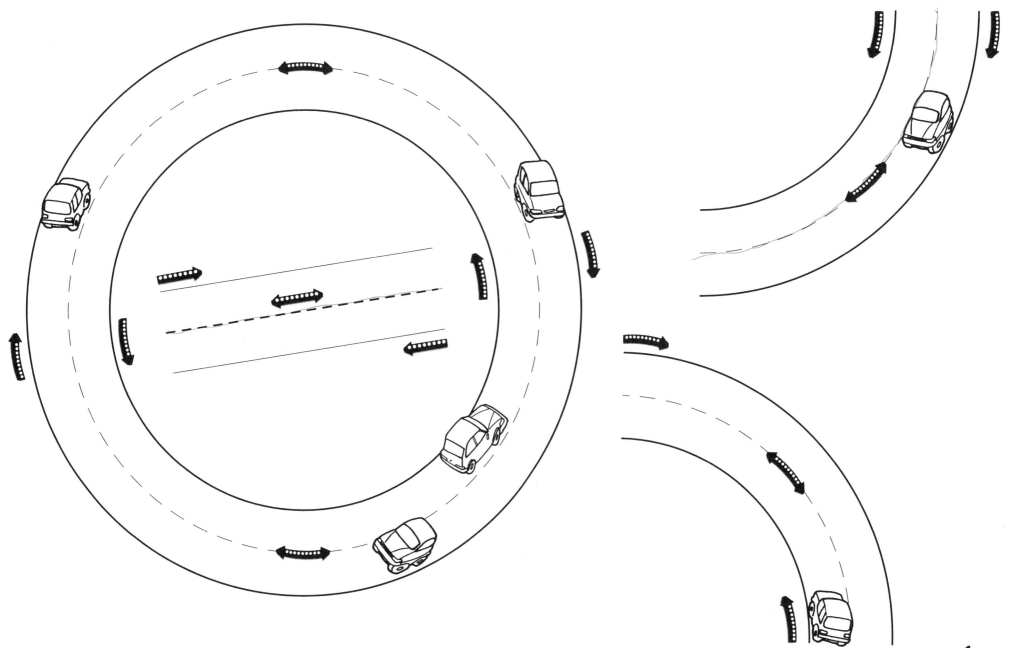

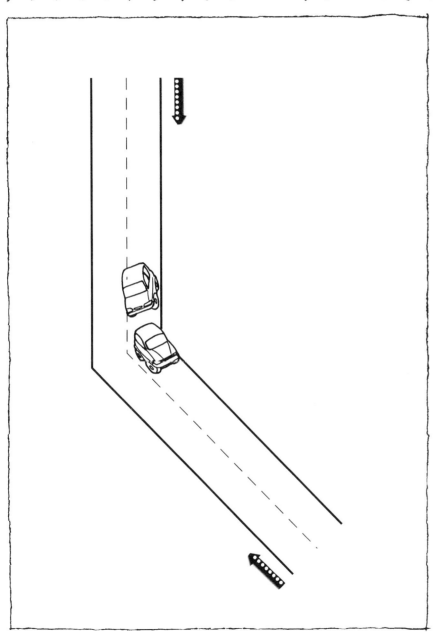

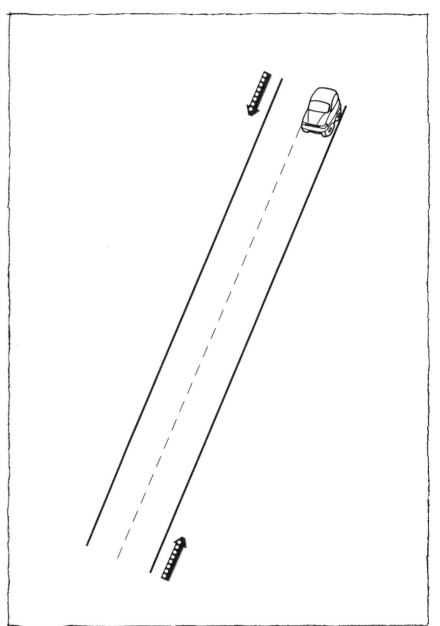

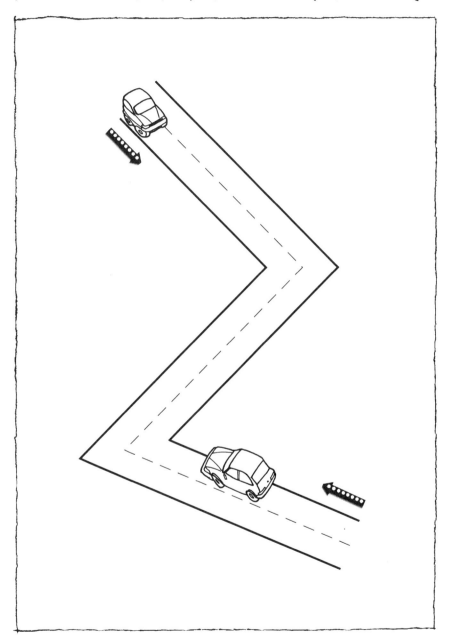

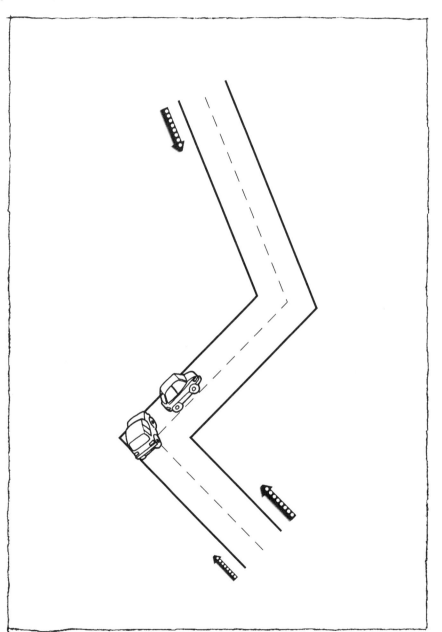

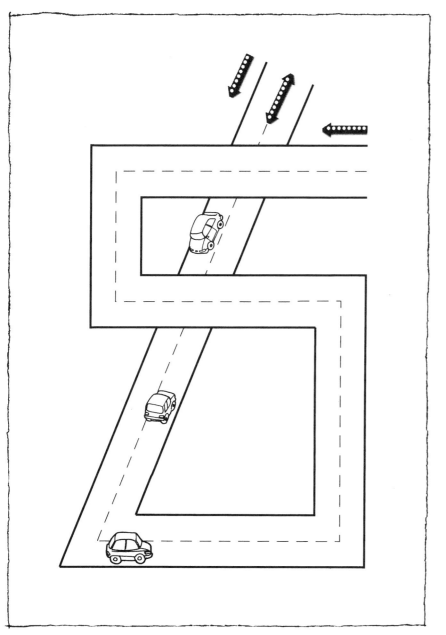

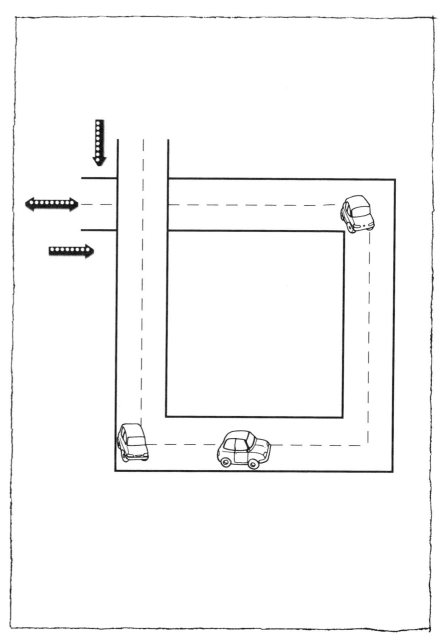

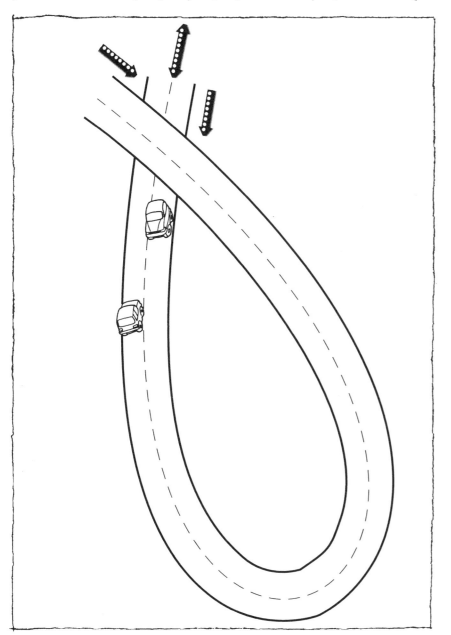

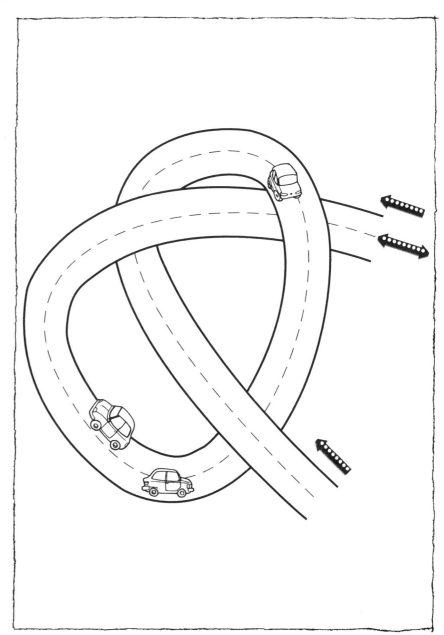

Booklet 4

B. Fluency
Booklet pages 6–15

The following tasks stretch the child's pencil control further whilst developing their orientation and fluency. The child must add the 'petals' to the flowers travelling in the direction indicated by the arrow and without removing their pencil from the page. How the child struggles with the dilemma of maintaining a pattern whilst the orientation alters, necessitating the shape to be reversed and inverted is complex indeed.

In this exercise you may find the child's physical posture changing, their wrists twisting, books turning, etc., as they attempt the challenge.

The child can add a smile to the flower's face if they feel the task has been successfully accomplished. The child should also be encouraged to see how the shape practised can represent certain letters such as *m*, *n* & *w*.

The letters can be shown in the context of a word and the child encouraged to try to reproduce them. For example;

The orientation changes are necessary in handwriting because the production of *c* and *d* involves movement in an anticlockwise direction whilst the letters *m*, *n*, & *h* and the numeral 3 involve movement in a clockwise direction.

The extension using squares and triangles furthers the understanding of form and introduce new dilemmas for the child to tackle. Control is extended by introducing zigzag shapes. This develops the skills required when producing capital letters *M*, *W*, *V*, *N*, & *Z* although it is stressed that these are not joining letters.

Mary

Newcastle

William

m   mum   _____

w   worm   _____

n   nose   _____

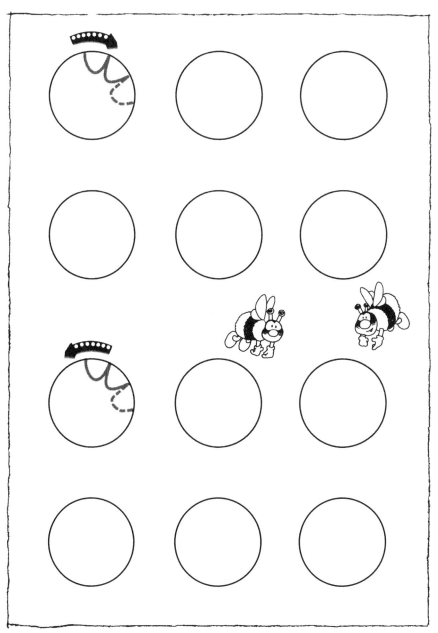

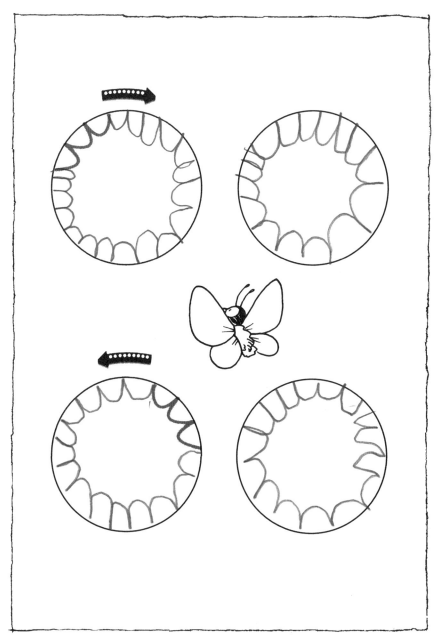

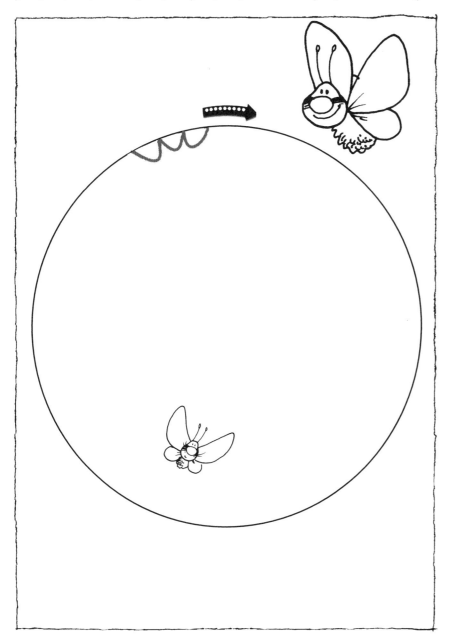

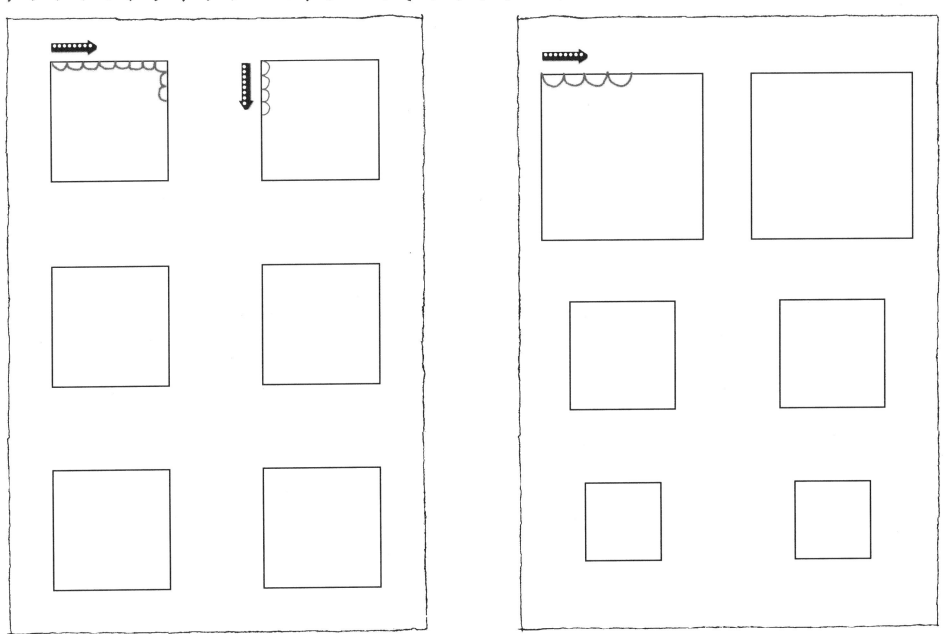

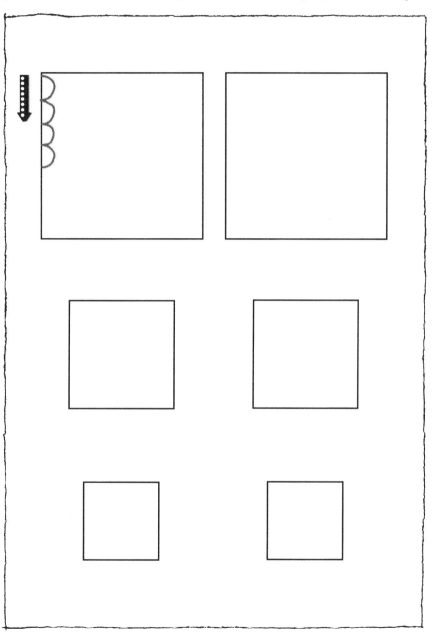

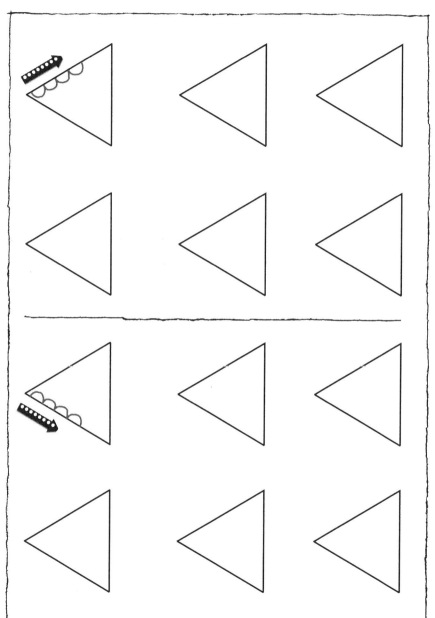

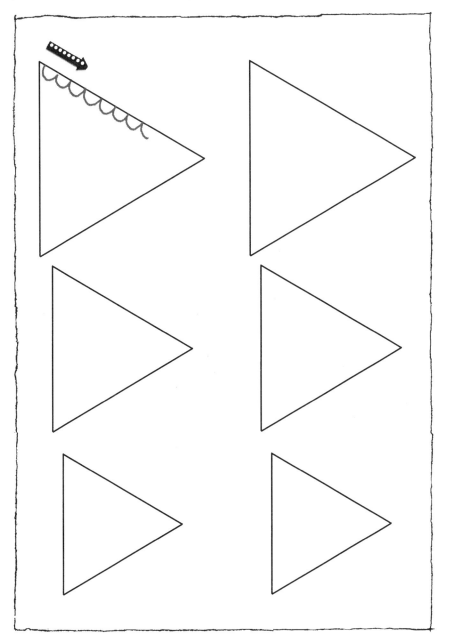

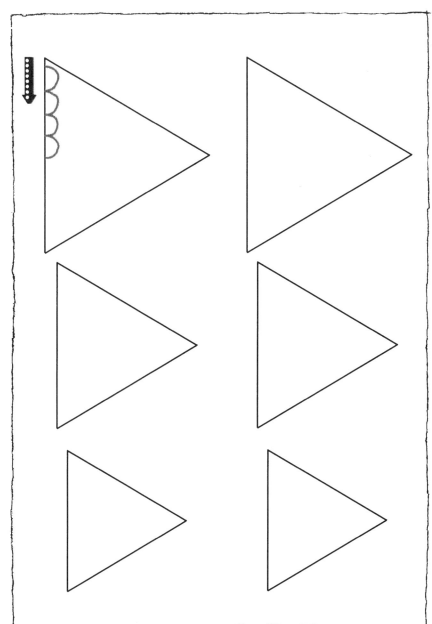

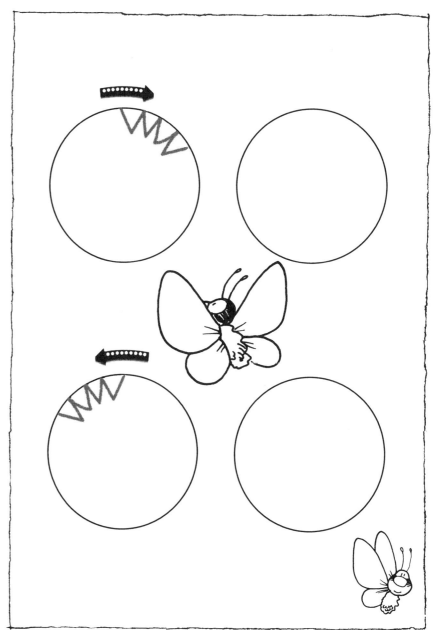

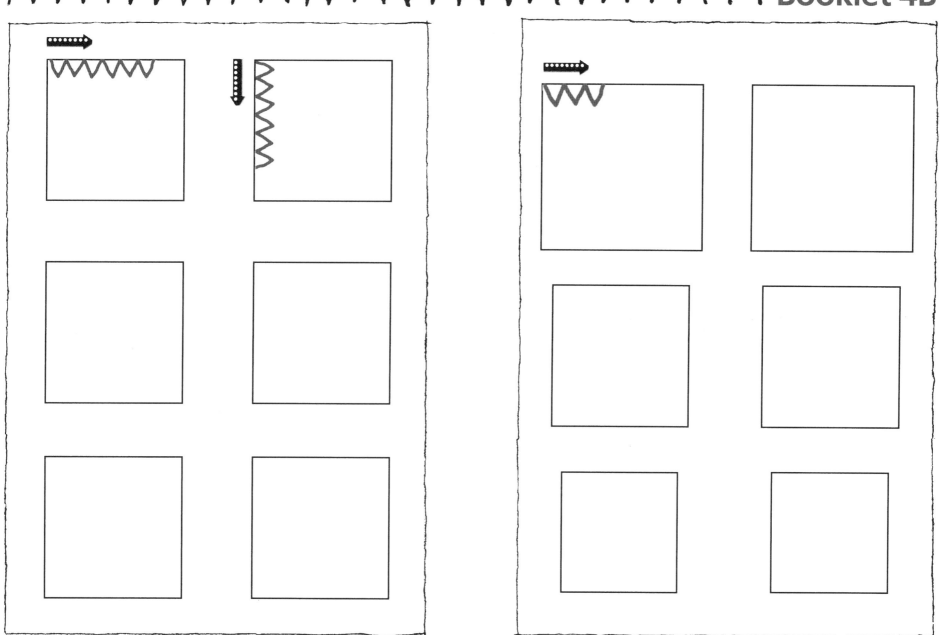

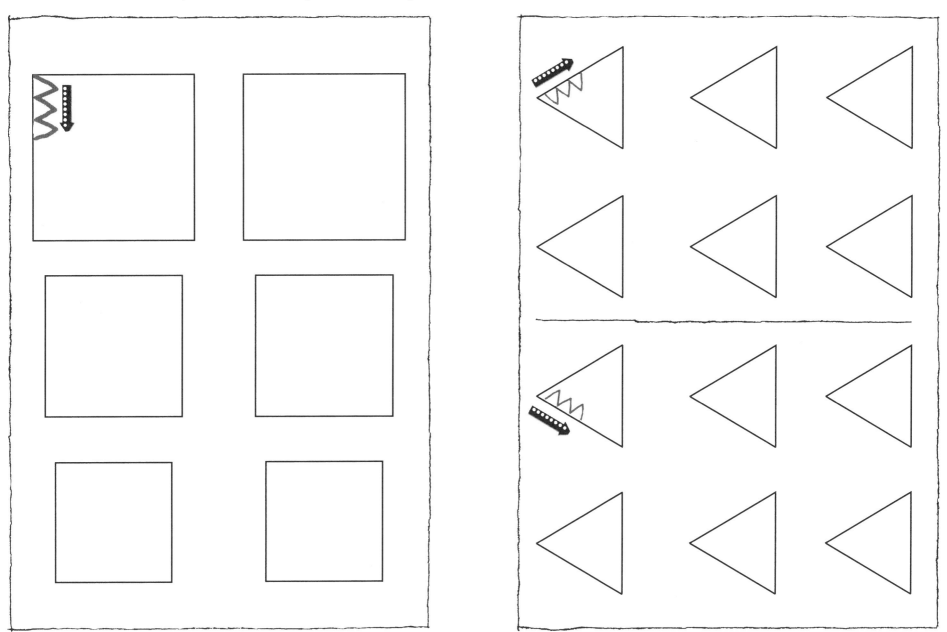

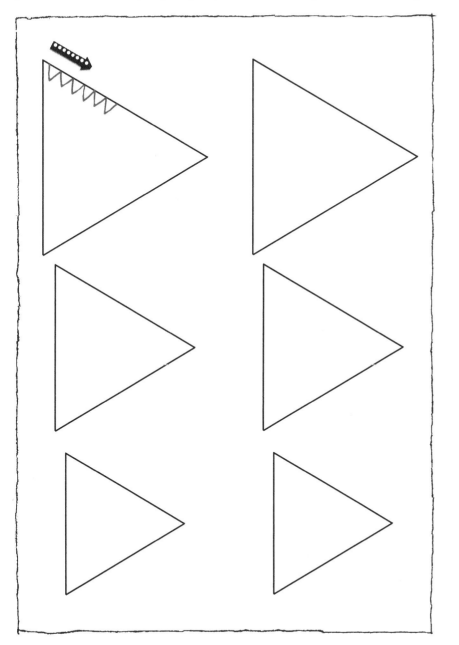

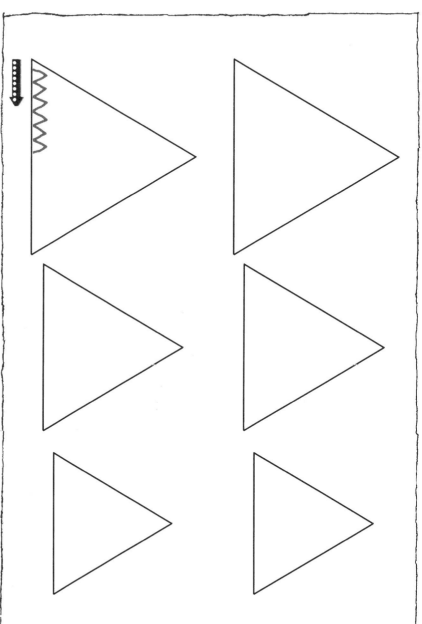

Booklet 4

C. Understanding size
Booklet pages 16–32
Additional worksheets 33–36

The following series of exercises elaborate on the previous tasks. 'Fences' are placed at equal distances around the given shape, whether a circle, square or triangle. These fences are to be jumped over and should not be used as starting or finishing points, nor as pointers to judge the size of the 'petals'.

The child learns how to see equidistant spaces around the given shape and must monitor every movement of the pencil to not only span the fence successfully and land on the shape's outline, but also to organise orientation, direction and fluency, eventually producing evenly-placed petals on a uniform flower.

The object of this exercise is to develop the child's understanding of size, appreciating that some letters are small, some are large and others are long. By producing similar petals in either small or large form, a useful discussion can take place regarding the differentiation of letter size when writing and its effects on legibility.

At a later stage letter patterns can be differentiated, and practice can be given in their formation. Games can also be played with the child to reinforce this difference, examples of which can be seen towards the end of the exercises.

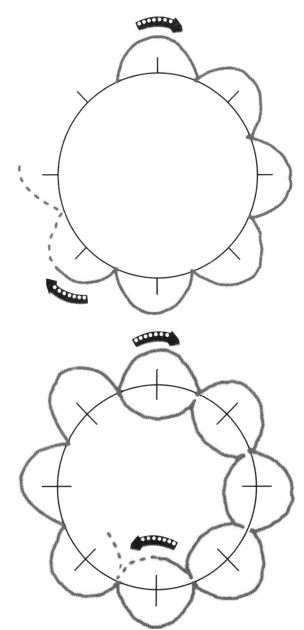

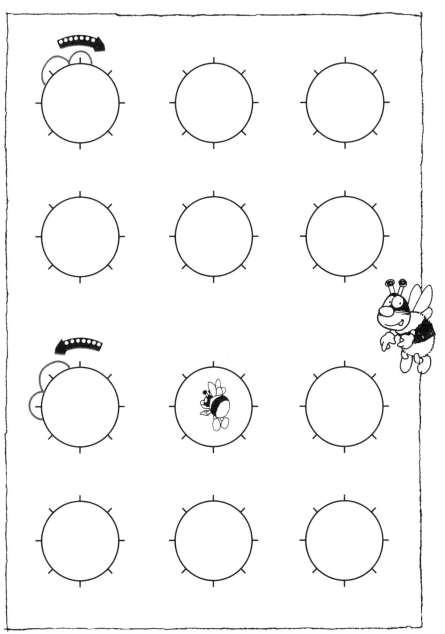

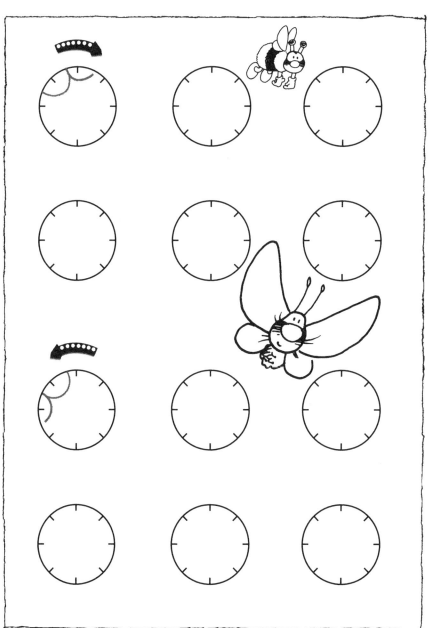

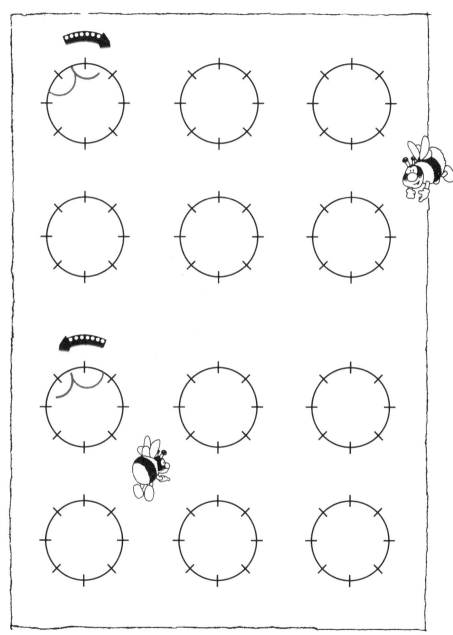

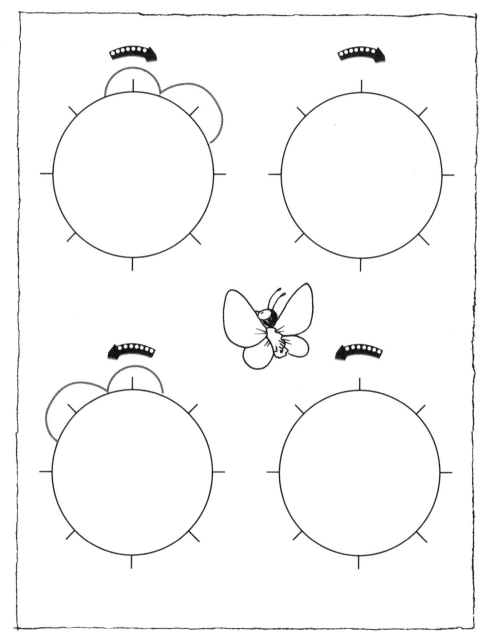

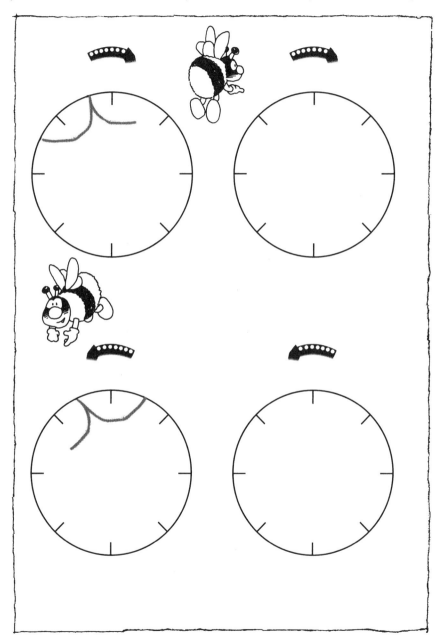

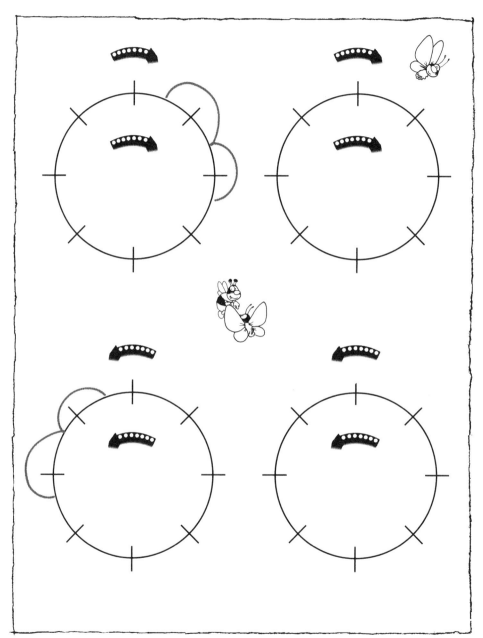

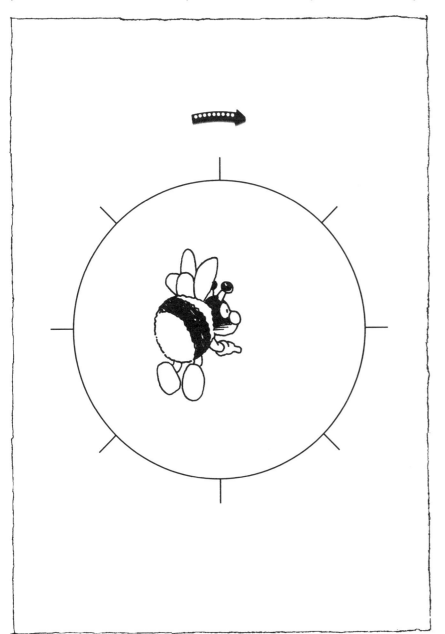

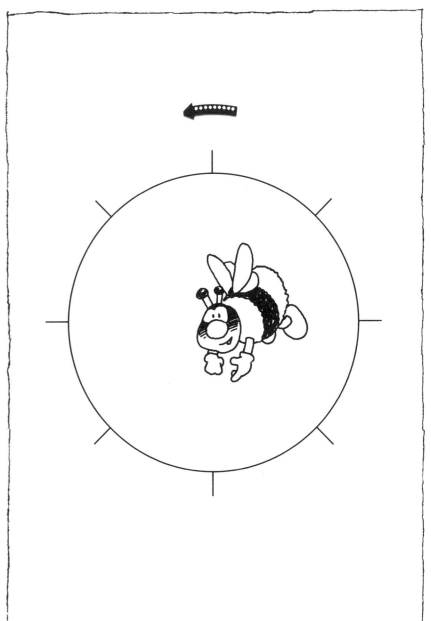

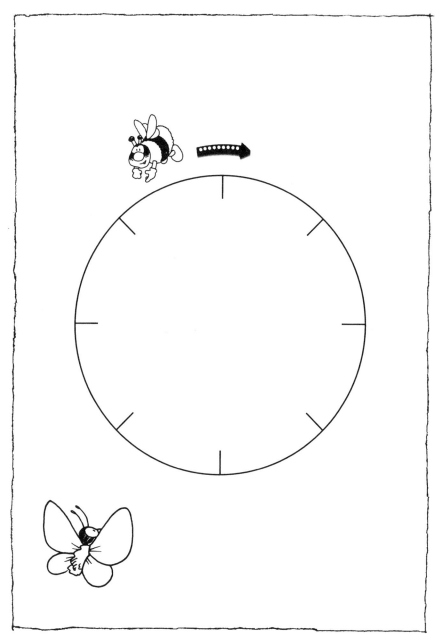

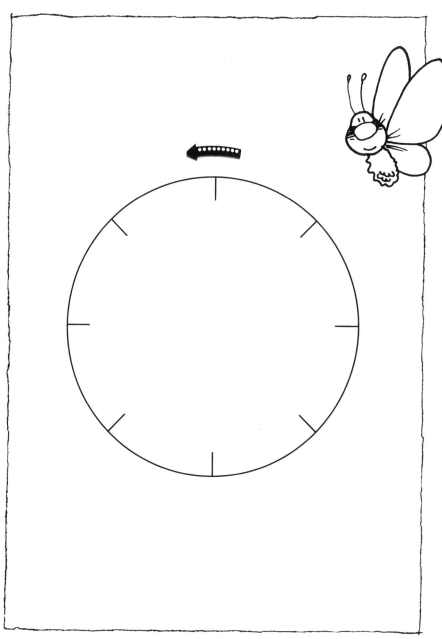

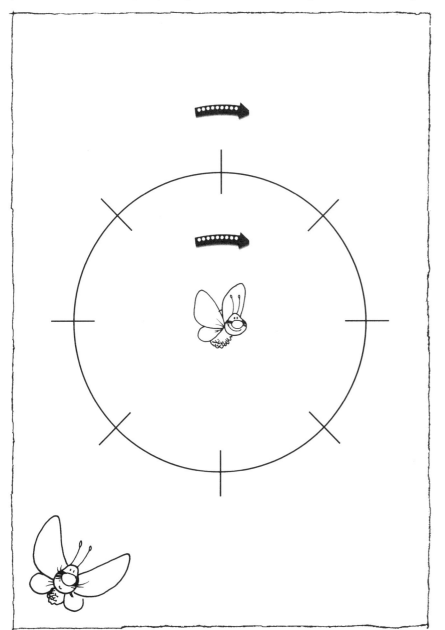

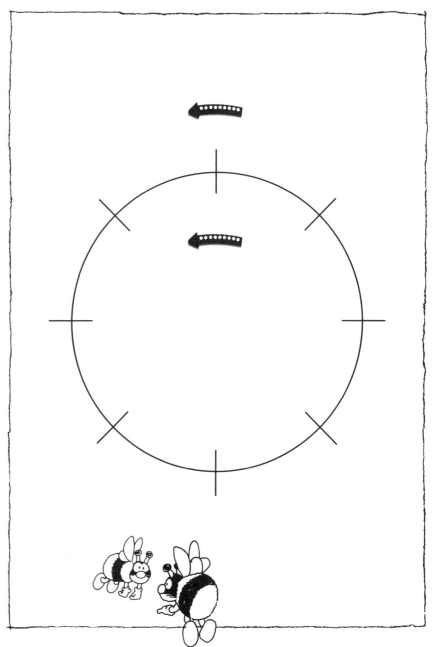

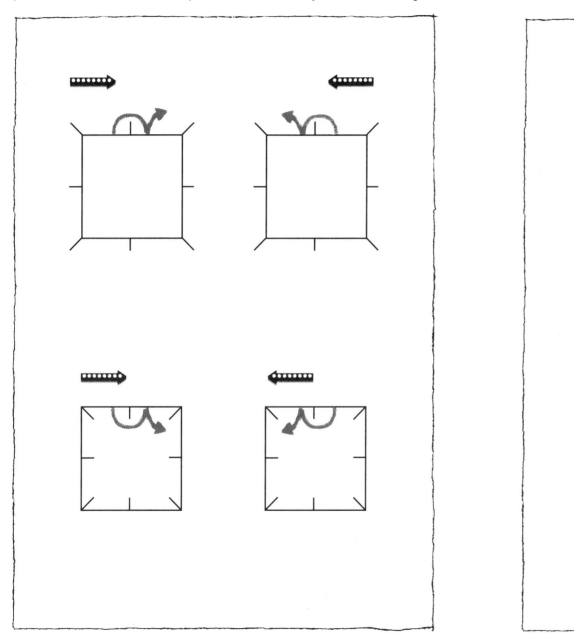

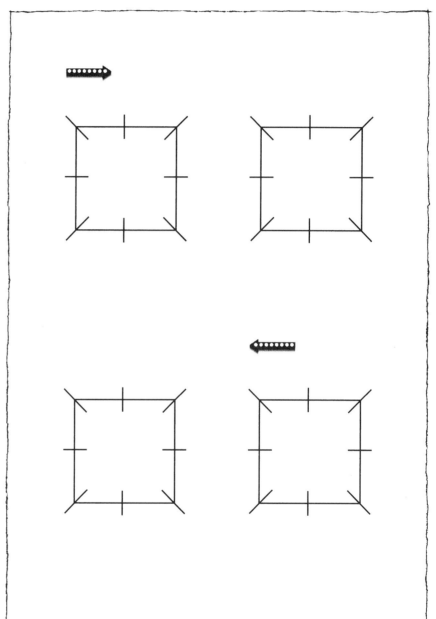

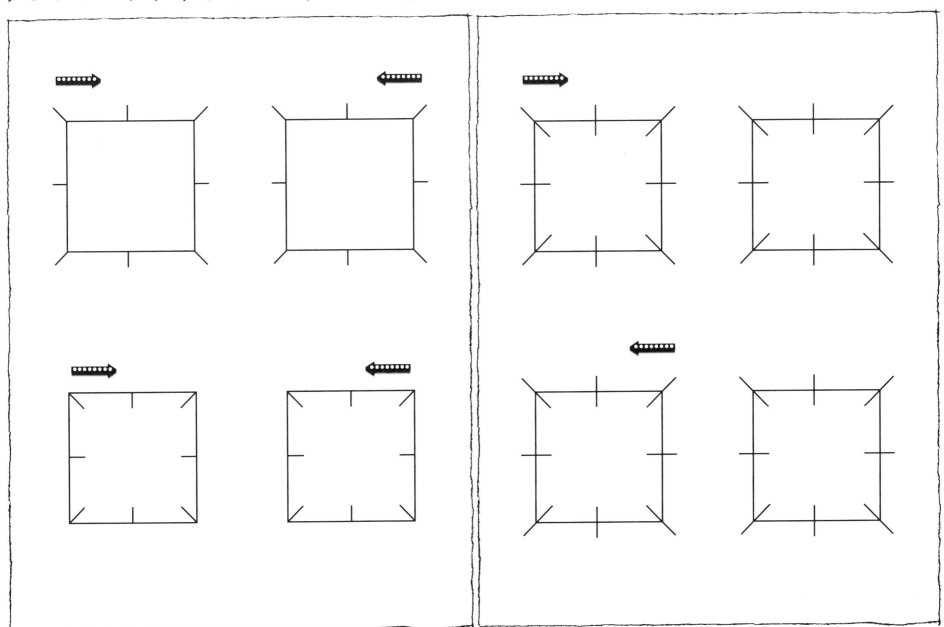

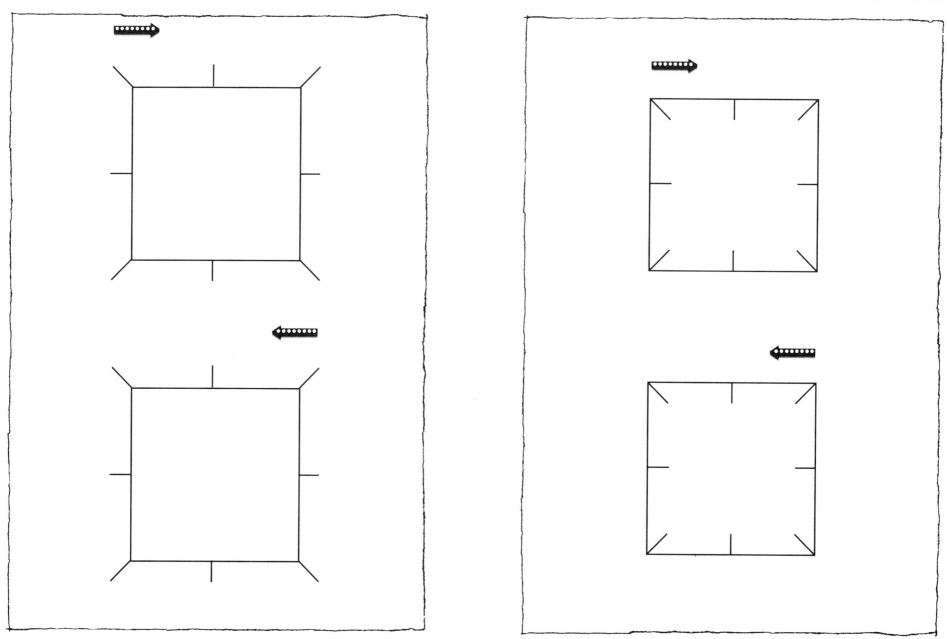

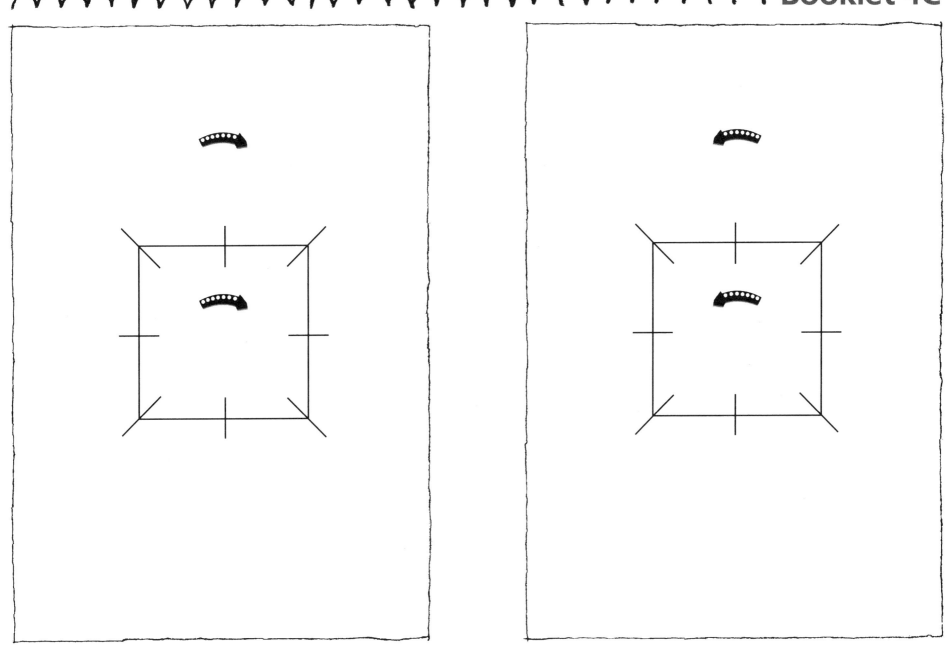

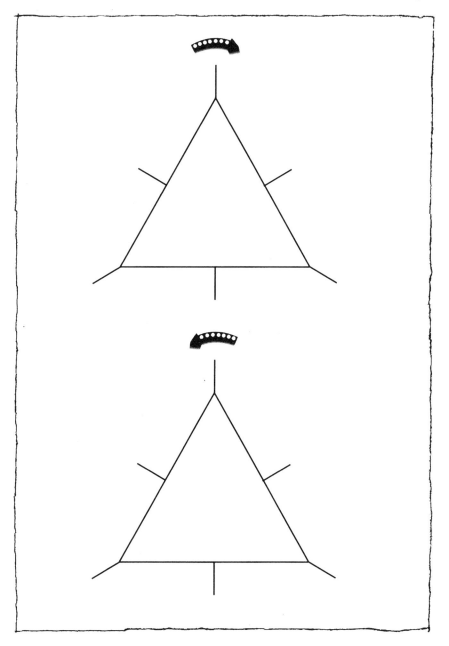

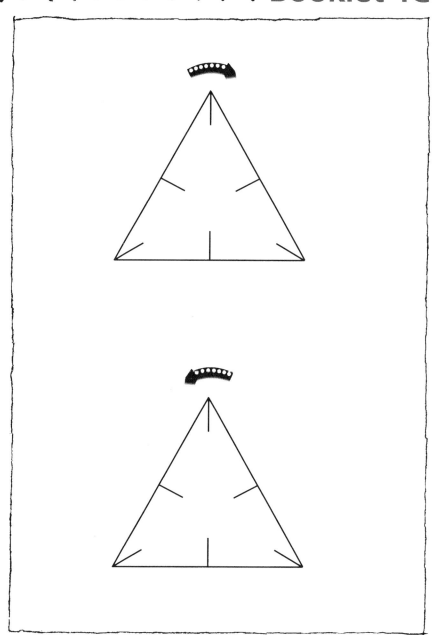

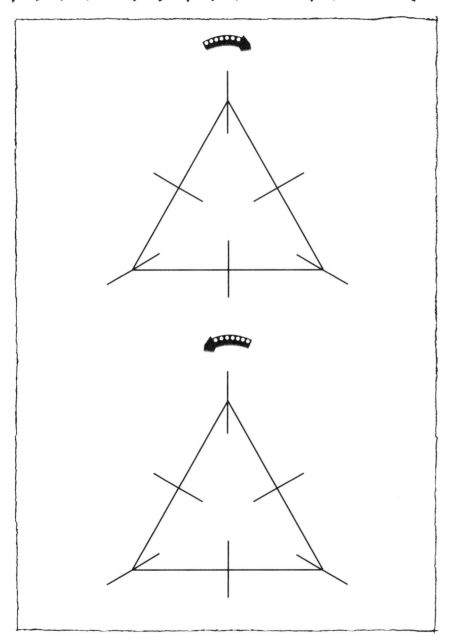

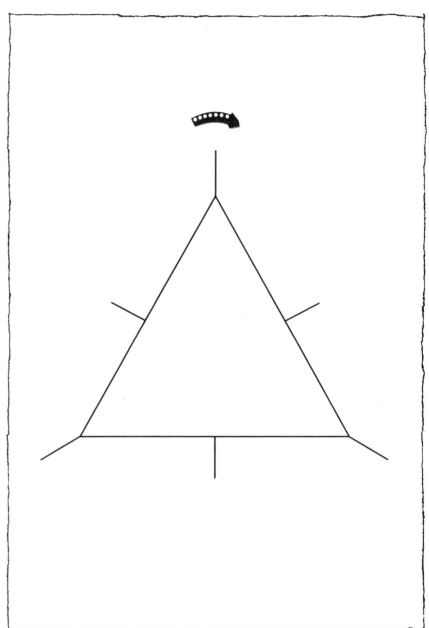

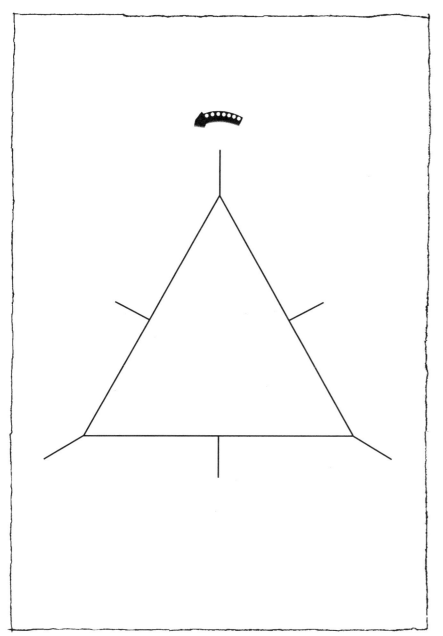

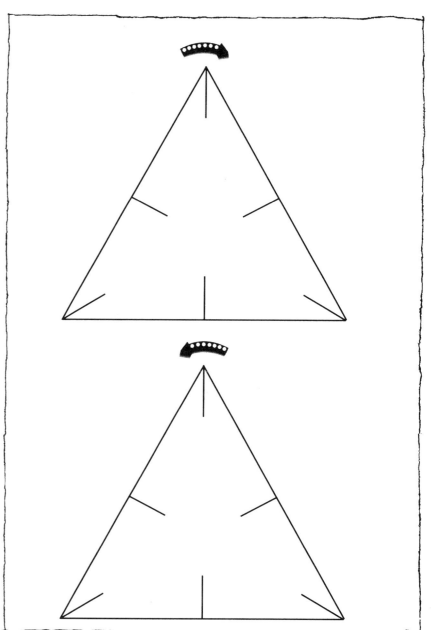

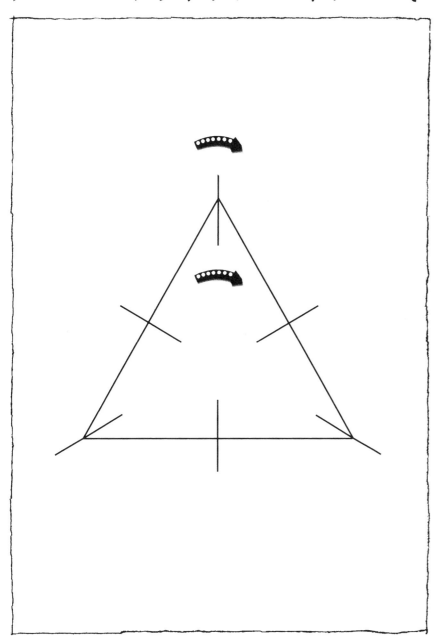

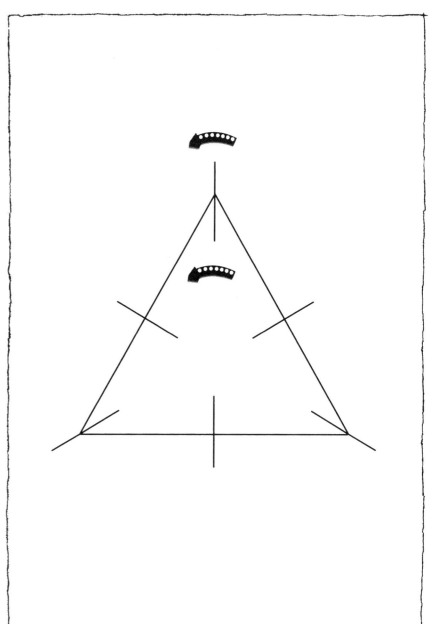

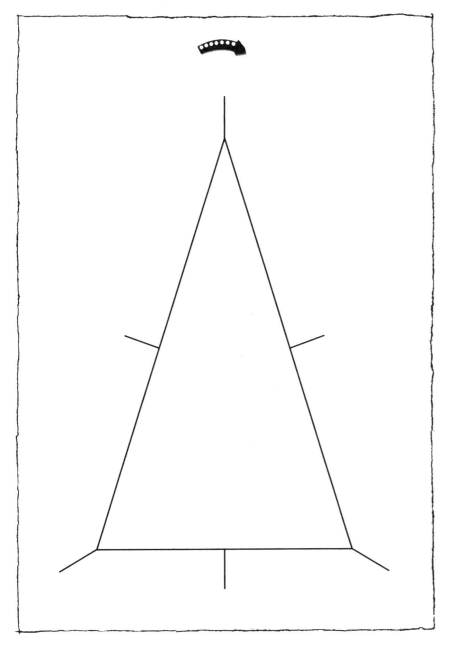

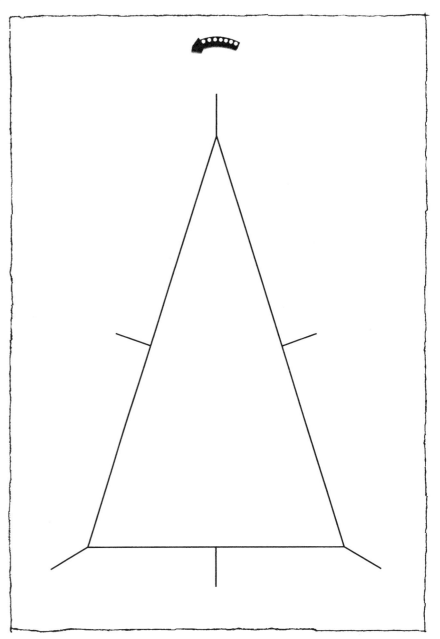

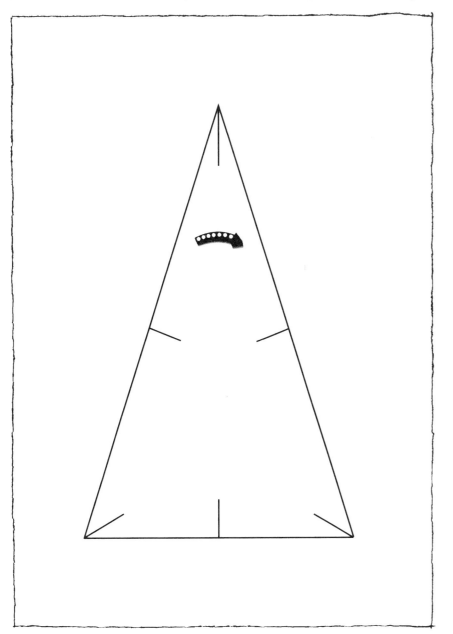

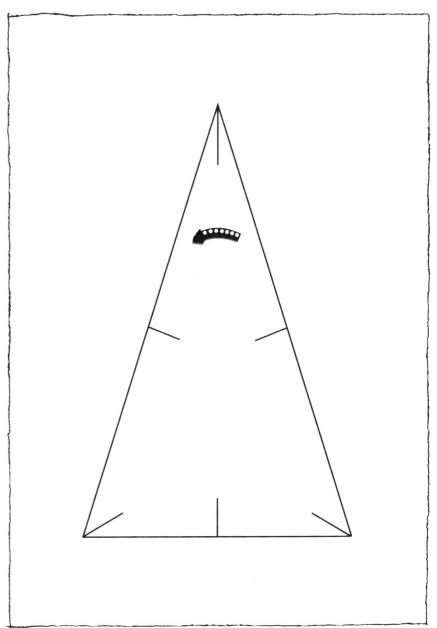

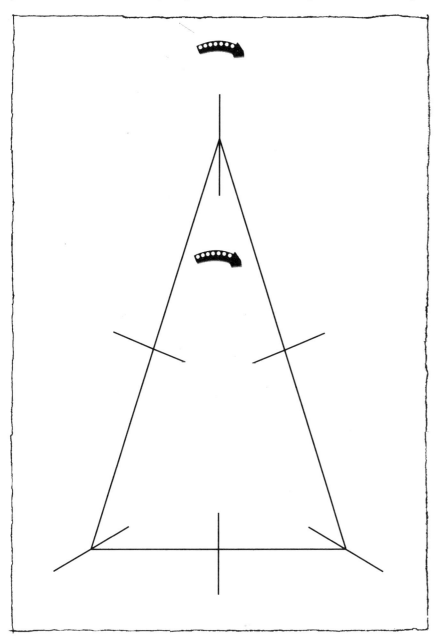

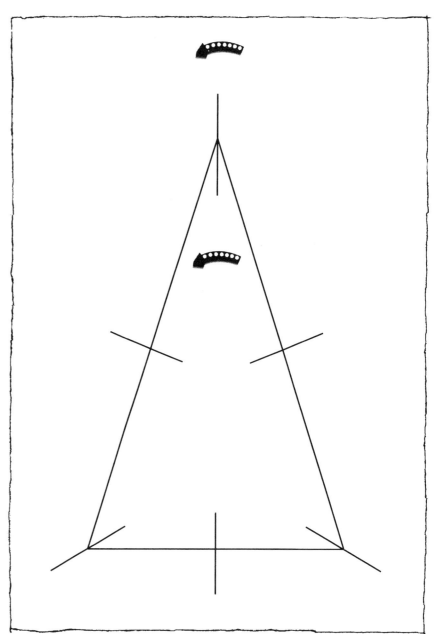

Draw a circle around all the little letter **a**s and **e**s you can find in this sentence.

The quick brown fox jumped over the lazy dog.

Can you find all the little letter **o**s and **c**s in this sentence?

I have a pet dog. His name is Harold. He is a King Charles spaniel and has beautiful soft floppy ears and a golden coat.

Can you find all the little letter **i**s and **r**s in this sentence?

Tara and her friend Tim lived in the same street and walked to school together each day.

Can you find all the little letter **u**s and **w**s in this sentence?

The weather today is wet, windy and cold. I think I shall stay indoors and curl up in front of a warm fire with a story book and dream of sunny days.

Draw a circle around all the tall letter **b**s and **t**s you can find in this sentence.

The quick brown fox jumped over the lazy dog.

Can you find all the tall letter **d**s and **t**s in this sentence?

I have a pet dog. His name is Harold. He is a King Charles spaniel and has beautiful soft floppy ears and a golden coat.

Can you find all the tall letter **d**s and **h**s in this sentence?

Tara and her friend Tim lived in the same street and walked to school together each day.

Can you find all the tall letter **l**s and **t**s in this sentence?

The weather today is wet, windy and cold. I think I shall stay indoors and curl up in front of a warm fire with a story book and dream of sunny days.

Draw a circle around all the long letter **q**s and **j**s you can find in this sentence.

The quick brown fox jumped over the lazy dog.

Can you find all the long letter **g**s and **p**s in this sentence?

I have a pet dog. His name is Harold. He is a King Charles spaniel and has beautiful soft floppy ears and a golden coat.

Can you find all the long letter **g**s and **y**s in this sentence?

Tara and her friend Tim lived in the same street and walked to school together each day.

Can you find all the long letter **y**s and **f**s in this sentence?

The weather today is wet, windy and cold. I think I shall stay indoors and curl up in front of a warm fire with a story book and dream of sunny days.

f	c	j	d	j	h	i	j	l	g
a	b	f	e	f	g	k	j	g	m
y	j	w	f	t	j	s	g	o	n
z	x	v	j	u	f	r	q	p	q
y	b	g	c	y	d	f	z	p	g
a	g	f	f	g	e	y	g	p	b
j	i	y	h	j	t	j	a	p	c
j	k	j	g	s	f	x	q	f	d
l	m	f	q	r	u	w	f	e	g
f	n	o	p	p	v	f	g	g	h

a	i	u	h	i	k	e	j	m	e
b	u	a	g	a	e	l	u	e	o
c	u	f	e	p	i	o	u	a	n
d	a	e	q	a	r	a	i	u	e
s	e	t	i	y	o	z	u	a	i
u	v	w	x	a	u	g	i	b	c
e	i	l	i	e	h	i	f	o	d
n	m	a	o	k	j	o	a	o	e
a	o	e	p	a	s	u	a	z	a
u	e	r	q	o	t	v	w	x	y

Letter Search

Can you find all the long letters? (These are all the letters which hang down under a line.)

f	g	j	p	q	y

Can you find all the letters which are vowels?

a	e	i	o	u